The Girls' Life
Awesome
Advice Guide
to Everything

Written by "Dear Carol"
a.k.a. Carol Weston

Illustrated by John & Wendy

Scholastic Inc.

New York • Toronto • London • Auckland • Sydney
Mexico City • New Delhi • Hong Kong • Buenos Aires

ISBN 0-439-44977-4

Copyright © 2003 by Girls' Life Magazine

Design: Mark Neston
Illustrations © John and Wendy

All rights reserved. Published by Scholastic Inc.

SCHOLASTIC and associated logos are trademarks and/or registered trademarks of Scholastic Inc.

12 11 10 9   6 7 8/0

Printed in the U.S.A.

First Scholastic printing, February 2003

Contents

The Girls' Life Awesome Advice Guide to Everything

Dear Reader

Ever wonder what other girls your age wonder about? Need some straight-ahead advice about growing up, friendship, boys, and family? Looking for comfort or common sense? Check out these Q's and A's, and you'll find your issues addressed here.

It's good when a girl can talk to her friends about her crush and to her mom about her body. But not all girls can comfortably do that, and even if they *could*, it can still help to get a second opinion. That's one reason why so many girls have written to me over the past 18 years and why I think you'll like this book. Even if you don't happen to be bursting with any particular questions of your own, reading about other girls' concerns can give you insights that just might help you understand your friends and your own life.

The Girls' Life Awesome Advice Guide to Everything includes hundreds of letters from girls just like you. Some readers have asked me if the questions are real. Yes! I've got stacks of mail on every topic, so there's no need to make them up. Who are the letters from? Girls who feel left out or worried, girls whose friends are acting weird or annoying, girls with boyfriends, girls without boyfriends, and girls getting used to non-traditional families. This book reflects my mail, and my mail reflects what's on girls' minds—maybe even yours.

You can start this book at the beginning, or jump in anywhere, based on the topics. You can also read these letters out loud with a friend and discuss the advice. The book is organized by subject, and covers all the normal girlhood stresses and messes. It begins with how to be your best self, and then moves on to chapters about your body, new and old friends, crushes and boyfriends, and stuff surrounding growing up and family matters.

The questions here can give you perspective and the answers can give you tools. Maybe you'll think, "At least I'm not like that!" or, "Huh, I never thought of complimenting my stepdad," or, "Well, here goes, I'm going to tell my friend why I'm feeling hurt." *The Girls' Life Awesome Advice Guide to Everything* shows that almost everyone goes through rocky times, and that almost every situation can be improved.

Do you usually feel pretty good about things? I hope so. But if you sometimes feel worried or off balance, know that every confident woman was once a confused girl. You don't have to be in a crisis to confide in an adult or talk over issues with your friends. You can check out the exclusive website for *GL* club members only, at www.scholastic.com/girlslife for advice and information. You can also send letters and questions to me at Dear Carol, GL, 4517 Harford Road, Baltimore, MD 21214. Be sure to include a self-addressed stamped envelope for a reply, and check future *GL* magazines to see if your letter makes it into my column.

I bet you're good to your friends—so be good to yourself, too! Take care of your body, work hard, have fun, and do your best to get along with your family. If you are sensitive and sensible, things really *will* go your way. You'll see!

Wishing you the best!

Love,
Carol

Chapter 1

"Try to feel good about what
you have, instead of feeling
bad about what you don't."

W ho are you? What do you like best about yourself? What do you wish you could change?

Sure, it would be great to be a confident student, a sought-after friend, an athlete-artist with a cool room that stays magically clean and organized. It would also be nice to feel happy all the time—but who fits *that* description?

Are you sometimes moody? Do you sometimes feel jealous, shy, overwhelmed, or left out? Join the club!

You're a wonderful person. But you're not a *perfect* person, because there's no such thing. So don't be too hard on yourself for being human. Just keep striving to be in charge of your life. This chapter can help you find your strengths, make sense of your moods, speak up and be heard, and feel good about becoming your very best self.

Making the grade

Dear Carol,

I have never been on the honor roll and I need advice on how to get better grades. What should I be doing?

—C Student

Dear C Student,

After school every day, set yourself up in a quiet, well-lit place, and plow through your work, subject by subject. Take mini breaks to rejuvenate, but not mega ones. Instead of passively reading textbooks, grab a pencil or highlighter and underline key sentences, or take notes. That way, you'll be studying *actively* so the info has a better chance of sinking into your brain—and staying there. Can your folks help you prepare for your vocabulary or spelling tests? Or perhaps you can get a study buddy or a tutor. Don't let yourself get behind, seek help from teachers when you need it, and choose at least one subject to shine in. You really *can* become a better student.

Dear Carol,

All my life, my friends and I have been made fun of for being good students. We're called geeks and nerds just because we get good grades and do well on tests. Part of the problem is that we're all in the same gifted and talented class, and other kids see that as snobby. My mom says they're jealous. What can I do?

—A-nnoyed Student

Dear A-nnoyed,

Make sure that you're mingling with kids in other classes, and that you're friendly—and never condescending. Can you audition for a play, or join an after-school club or sport that could help you meet other girls? Once you start getting to know others, can you call someone up and go shopping or to a movie? How about throwing a party or having a sleepover? I bet you have it in you to be not just gifted and talented academically, but gifted and talented with others, too!

Dear Carol,

Next year I'm going to a very advanced school. I'm trying to study harder, but I have this friend who keeps talking to me and writing me notes during class. What should I do to make her stop, without hurting her feelings?

—Trying Hard

Dear Trying,
It's wonderful that you want to be a better student. The more you put into school, the more you'll get out of it. As for your friend, if you yell, "Quit bugging me!" you'll hurt her feelings. But if you politely say, "I have to pay attention if I'm going to do well on this test. Let's talk after class or sit together at lunch," she'll probably give you a break.

Dear Carol,

My friends all mock me whenever I use what they consider to be a big word. Today I said it was "stifling" out, and they nearly died laughing.

—Smart Kid

Dear Smart,
Your friends may be laughing because they feel insecure and embarrassed about not knowing the meaning of something you said. They may even envy your vocabulary—though they'd never admit it. Keep expressing yourself as well as you can. Being articulate without being a show-off is a talent—and smart kids often have the last laugh.

Hey, what about me?

Dear Carol,

These girls in my school are really preppy, live in really cool, big houses, and wear all new clothes. They are nice to me, but sometimes I think they're laughing at me behind my back.

—Not As Fortunate

Dear Not As Fortunate,
It can be hard when other girls have bigger houses or newer clothes than you do. But no matter how much you have, there is always someone out there who has more. So rather than dwell on comparisons and what *others* have, you're better off looking at what *you* have. Do you have a loving family? Are you rich in friends? What are your special talents? You say you are not as fortunate, but money is not the only form of measurement. And I doubt these girls are laughing at you any more than you would laugh at a girl whose house is smaller than yours!

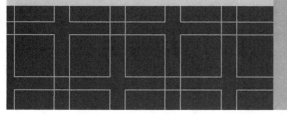

Dear Carol,

I'm getting jealous of my best friend. She gets an allowance and I don't.

—Jealous of Her

Dear Jealous,
Comparisons and jealousies are natural, but the challenge is to try to feel good about what you *have* instead of feeling bad about what you *don't*. That doesn't mean you can't ask your parents for an allowance. You can! But don't say you want an allowance because everyone else gets one. Explain that since you're older, you think it would be good for you to be responsible for a little of your own money. Are your folks still hesitant to hand you cash? Maybe they'll give you a few dollars each week if you do a few chores—take out the trash, put away the dishes, clean the hamster cage, whatever. Can't hurt to ask!

Dear Carol,

All of my friends have kissed or have been kissed by someone. I've never even been pecked on the lips. When we start talking about being kissed, I have nothing to say. Whenever my chance comes, I get scared. Should I tell my friends I feel embarrassed?

—Eleven and Never Been Kissed

Dear Never Been Kissed,

Most eleven-year-olds have never been kissed. Even a few of your kiss-and-tell friends are probably less experienced than they say. It's smart that you haven't rushed to kiss the first boy who puckers up— because a first kiss means more when you share it with someone you really like and who really likes you back. Next time everyone is talking about kissing, ask some questions, smile, or just sigh and light-heartedly say, "My time will come." You could even switch the subject to something else—but don't make up any stories. Your own first kiss may be just around the corner, so be patient!

Dear Carol,

Most of my friends dress up every day. They curl their hair and wear mini skirts, makeup, and perfume. One of my best buds colors her hair strawberry blond. Everything she wears has to be name-brand. Whenever I see my friends, they stare at me like I'm an ugly little nobody.

—Nobody

Dear Nobody (*Not*),

I'm sorry you feel stared-at and unattractive. Some girls brush their hair endlessly, wear the latest trends, and gob on makeup. Others go for a more natural, clean look. There are lots of ways to look good. If your friends choose to dress up, fine. If they belittle you because you don't dress like they do, they aren't really friends. Are you sure they are dissing you, or could you be feeling overly self-conscious? If it's the latter, is there a way to improve your appearance? Can you splurge on an outfit on sale? Can you ask a well-dressed cousin to give you her outgrown clothes? Can you sweet-talk a grandma into taking you for a haircut? As for attitude, you're *not* a nobody and you *can* distinguish yourself without coloring your hair. Are you a good reader? Rider? Painter? Dancer? Who you are on the inside matters *more* than what you wear or how you look. With some effort, you can feel like a swan instead of an ugly duckling.

Dear Carol,

I'm going into eighth grade and I have a lot of friends at school. But during weekends and vacations, no one wants to hang out with me. I never get calls from anyone.

—Lonely

Dear Lonely,

It's no fun to be lonely, so make some calls yourself. Don't just say, "Want to come over?" Say, "I rented a great video," or "Let's go to a movie," or "Want to go swimming?" or "We have an extra ticket to the concert," or "Want to come over to make cookies?" And don't just call random girls from your class. Think about which friends you like the most, which ones like you, and which ones live the closest.

Dear Carol,

All I can think of is how uncool I am. I have tried everything—journal writing, art, music...nothing works. All my friends are known around school for something (great violinist, incredible gymnast, artistic genius). Me? I'm the unspecial kid who shows up for class and disappears in the corner.

—The Lone Ranger

Dear Lone Ranger,

Tons of kids feel uncool and alone at times—even great violinists and incredible gymnasts. It's time to quiet the negative voice inside you and practice talking to yourself as you would talk to a friend. Don't say, "You're uncool." Say, "Way to go," or "That was great," or "You're off to a good start." Trust me—one day, you will figure out what your strengths and interests are. For now, ask yourself which is your best subject. Spanish? Science? Social studies? Really apply yourself in that course. Sit up front, take detailed notes, review your homework before class, and become a stronger student. Get involved in stage crew, photography club, or some other activity to lift you out of your doldrums. Still feeling bleak? Talk things over with your folks or a favorite relative. The middle-school years are hard for lots of girls and, then—hallelujah!—things really *do* get easier!

Dear Carol,

My regular baby-sitter has two kids, and they always tease and taunt me. I try to be nice to them but it always backfires, and I'm glad to go home. They also have lots of games, but they're always playing with them so I never get to.

—Sad and Mad

Dear Sad and Mad,

That stinks! If your parents are paying someone to look after you, that person's job is not only to make sure you are safe, but also not sad or mad. Talk to your parents (or even your baby-sitter) as calmly as you can, and tell them why the arrangement isn't working for you. Are there other baby-sitters around? Does your school offer after-school activities? Your sitter's two kids may be threatened by you because they don't like watching their mom dote on someone else. But that's her job, so if she isn't helping you feel welcome, then something's got to give.

Popularity problems

Dear Carol,

I'm in the cool clique and I'm in charge of it. A few days ago, a dork asked if she could join in. One girl said to give her a chance, and another said, "No way!" and the rest just want me to decide.

—Cool Clique

Dear C.C.,
You say you're in the cool clique, but the coolest people I know are warm and accepting of others. You want people to think highly of you, but you need to think well of yourself, too. You wouldn't have written to me if you were 100 percent comfortable with the whole exclusivity setup. Maybe it's time to think about disbanding the clique. Friendship should be about relationships between individuals—not walls around groups.

Dear Carol,

I'm in sixth grade and want to be popular. This girl Sarah is really nice, but she always has a book in her hand. Popular kids don't like her, but I know we would be great friends. Should I be her friend or be popular?

—Which One

Dear Which One,
There's no guarantee that by *wanting* to be popular, you *will* be popular. But if you think Sarah could be a great friend, what are you waiting for? It's better to have a few close friends than to be superficially popular. You can still be friendly to the popular kids without letting them keep you from being friends with others.

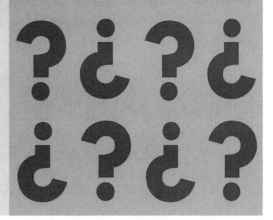

Dear Carol,
This guy at school gets teased big-time. I want to stick up for him, but I'm worried everyone will say that I am a dork, too.
—Dork Defender

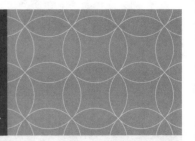

Dear Defender,
Surely you're not the only one with a heart. Pretty lame that you'd be labeled a dork just for being a decent person! Next time the rag session starts, say, "Oh, let's not make fun of him, poor guy," or, "I'm tired of talking about him," or, "Give him a break—he's not dorky on purpose." Try to introduce a new topic: a new movie or CD, the upcoming school dance, vacation plans, or how much homework the teachers have been inflicting on everyone. You don't have to become this boy's protector or best friend, but it's admirable that you want to skip the jest fest.

Dear Carol,

I'm popular in school and everything, but my big problem is my looks. I've inherited my grandfather's big, bushy, stuck-together eyebrows. I'm practically the only one in school with brows like this. My friends are nice about it, but others call me Brown Bear. How can I keep my confidence?

—Hairy

Dear Hairy,
I personally think it can be attractive to have a distinctive characteristic, whether it's a small scar, big brows, or a medium mole. Frida Kahlo (1907-1954) was a famous Mexican artist who often painted herself with one big beautiful brow. If you can learn to love your eyebrows, great! If not, talk to your mom about thinning them—maybe by tweezing or waxing. Either way, don't let a few big mouths shake your confidence. They don't deserve to have that power over you, so don't give it to them!

Argh! When people drive you crazy

Dear Carol,

This girl in my class thinks she is so cool. She thinks only her and her friends' clothes are in style. She acts just like she's Miss America. I get so annoyed! I'd like to smack her.

—Annoyed

Dear Annoyed,

Don't smack her—it won't change a thing and will only land you in the principal's office! I'm sure you're not the only one put off by this queen bee's snooty attitude, but stop letting it get to you. She's not losing sleep over you, so why lose sleep over her? Focus on your friends, activities, and, most of all, yourself. As you do more things to make yourself proud, you'll stop being so annoyed when she acts proud of herself!

Dear Carol,

I'm in fifth grade, and the only girl who lives on my street is in third grade. Every time I tell her I don't like something, she says, "I don't like it, either." Can't she make up her own mind?

—Sick of It

Dear Sick of It,

So, she looks up to you! There are worse crimes. As she gets older, she'll realize that people can be friends even when they have different opinions. If you find you're still impatient with her admiration, you can point out—kindly—that you'd like her even if she liked different stuff than you.

How to be your best

Dear Carol,

I've been playing flute since I was six, and now I'm thirteen. Everyone says I have talent, and I think I do, too. The problem? I can't make myself practice. My parents make me practice, but I never do it willingly. I'm auditioning for several big events this year, and practice makes perfect. But all the fun has gone out of it. I really need something to motivate me. Any ideas?
—Failing Flutist

Dear Flutist,
You're not a failing flutist—you're a *tired* flutist. Excellence in any field requires hard work, but maybe your parents would agree to a one-week respite from flute practice. If that doesn't work, you may need a change of tune. Can you join the school orchestra or form a jazz band with a friend or two? Can you ask your flute instructor if you can play a Dave Matthews song? Can you treat yourself *after* you practice? And how about those big events? Are you scared of blowing the auditions—or of acing them? If the flute just doesn't toot your horn anymore, find someone to talk to about this—if not your parents, perhaps your music teacher or a friend's mom. If it's music you love—just not the flute—consider taking lessons and learning to play a different instrument.

Dear Carol,

I have trouble talking at school. Everyone asks me, "Can you talk? How come you never talk?" I hate it, but I just can't find the courage to speak up.

—Quiet Girl in Desperate Need

Dear Quiet,

Can you practice yapping in comfy situations—like with a BFF or with your siblings? Can you flip through magazines and newspapers so you have something to contribute when conversation turns to music, movies, or fashion? Can you gab with cousins on the phone? Can you give yourself gold stars or some other little reward for raising your hand in school? You may never be an extrovert, but you'll be doing yourself a favor if you find the courage to speak up in class and to kids you like. What's the worst that could happen if you talked more? You may feel self-conscious. What's the worst that could happen if you don't? You may feel invisible and not find your way out of your, as you put it, "desperate need." It might even be helpful to try a public-speaking class!

Dear Carol,

People make fun of my weird name. I've tried to change it to something else, but it's not me. I've tried using a middle name or nickname, but I can't get used to that, either. My name has a short bad word in the middle, and people call me that bad word. I try to ignore them, but it hurts.

—Hurt

Dear Hurt,

When you're an adult, and your neighbors, friends, and coworkers are all grown up and mature, you'll probably have renewed pride in your unusual name. Meantime, kids can be mean, and you're in a bind. You can try pretending the teasing doesn't hurt because then, eventually, they'll stop. Or, you can tell your closest friends that the teasing *does* bother you because then, at least, those friends will stop. Or why not go by your initials? Ask your friends and teachers to call you by the initials of your first and last name or some creative combo. Initials often make great nicknames!

Dear Carol,

Ever since third grade I've had a reputation for being, well, weird. At least that's what everybody says. I'm in fifth grade now and don't want people to think I'm weird, so I mostly stick to myself. My friends think I should hang around other kids and just be myself. But it's kind of hard to be yourself when you don't fit in.

—Need Help

Dear Need Help,

Many girls feel confused about who they are and where they fit in. Although reputations can be hard to shake, it is possible to alter the way people think of you. I'm sure you're *not* weird. The thing is, the more you retreat from others, the more weird you'll seem. Think about what makes you *you*. Are you a good athlete, student, or pianist? If you want to change, do a few things differently. Join the track team, the band, or the student council. Dress in a way that's more—or less—eye-catching. One more idea: Talk to your parents about possibly going away to camp next summer, where you could start from scratch with a new group of kids. Making new friends may give your confidence a boost.

Dear Carol,

I'm shy and I'm sick of it! I can never think of anything to say to anybody. And when adults talk to me, I clam up even more. I'm worried people will think I'm snobby or boring. What can I do to seem friendlier?

—Wallflower

Dear Wallflower,

Many kids are shy, but you're right, people can mistake shyness for rudeness. Recognizing this is the first step to being bolder. If an adult asks, "How's school?" try not to mumble, "OK." Instead, say something like, "My favorite subject is English—we're reading a novel by Steinbeck," or describe what you like least about school. Keep the conversation going by asking if the person has read a book you liked, seen a movie you enjoyed, or has made plans for the long weekend or vacation ahead. If your mind goes blank, do what others do: Talk about the weather— chatting about the sky can get conversations off the ground!

Dear Carol,

I'm not incredibly shy, but whenever I'm around people I don't know very well, I get nervous and can't think of anything to say. If I do say something, it comes out all wrong. There are only a few girls I can really be myself around, and I've known them for years. The thing is, if girls get to know me, they like me, but most girls don't get the chance to know me.

—Allergic to People

Dear Allergic,
Tons of girls (and boys, for that matter) feel self-conscious at times. Fishing for something friendly and foolproof to say? Try a safe casual compliment such as, "I like your sandals," or, "Your science project was amazing." Or talk about the here-and-now: "It's so nice out!" or, "Isn't this pizza great?" If you wish you had more to talk about, become an expert on something. When you know a lot about a subject—whether it's cooking or computers—you can talk about it with confidence. Finally, the world needs good listeners as well as good talkers, and a lot of people will like you if what you have to say is mostly, "And then what happened?" or, "How was the movie? Did you like it?"

Dear Carol,

I'm really bossy. I'm so bossy my friends' parents talk about me. I don't mean to be. I'm afraid if I keep it up, I'll lose all my friends.

—Unexplainably Bossy

Dear Bossy,
Oh, dear. There are a few situations where you can get away with being bossy. But usually, bossiness wears thin. And you're right—if you're bossy, you run the risk of alienating everyone. Fortunately, you are wise enough to recognize your not-so-great tendency. Next time you're in the mood for plain pizza and everyone else votes pepperoni, don't protest. Just pick off the little round jobbies, and give yourself invisible gold stars for going with the flow. I'm not saying you should go from bulldozer to doormat. But you will be doing yourself (and your friends) a favor if you tune in to their feelings, too. Be open to other people's ideas, and you won't have to worry about losing your friends!

Dear Carol,
Sometimes when I'm alone, I talk to myself. Is this normal?
—Self Talker

Dear Self Talker,
It's OK to talk to yourself when you're alone. Many people say things to themselves like, "I can do this," or "I have nothing to wear!" or "Why hasn't he called?" or "I can't believe school's about to start." As long as your solo conversations are not long-winded, there's no reason to worry. On the other hand, try to rein it in a bit (since this habit bothers you). Why not consider talking to your diary instead? Diary writing is a great way to express your thoughts and feelings. Also, try to spend more time with friends—so your monologues can become dialogues!

You! New and improved

Dear Carol,
My room is an absolute disaster! My parents have had it with me and, though I hate to admit it, I feel trapped myself. How can I get it in order?
—Disaster Zone

Dear Disaster,
If you could see my office, you'd know that I could use some help in that department, too! When things get too messy, though, I sigh really loudly, take a deep breath, and force myself to clean up. I put on upbeat CDs, and I keep organizing until the music stops. The trick is not to get overwhelmed—but to get started and to get the job done, bit by bit. Sort the stuff on your desk or floor into three piles—put away, throw away, and give away. Same with drawers—dump a drawer on the floor or on a clean table and sort, sort, sort. Ready to tackle your closet? Select items that don't fit you anymore, or no longer look good, and give them to someone younger or to a charity. Stay at it all afternoon or just an hour a day for a week, and you'll be thrilled at how much better your room looks—and how much lighter you feel. Want some help clearing out the clutter? Ask a friend or sibling to help with your room this week, hers next. And then give yourselves a reward—like a new set of cool pens or a trip to get fruit smoothies.

Dear Carol,

I'm a computer/video-game/TV junkie. Every time I get in the zone, I become a zombie. I shut out my parents and friends, and they get really angry when they have to pull me away from the screen to talk. I want to save up for a Playstation or Nintendo 64, but I know my parents will find me glued to the screen 24/7. I really want to get over this bad habit.

—Screen Zombie

Dear Zombie,

Since you know you're too glued to the tube, forget your pursuit of Playstation or N64. It's easier to resist purchasing it than to resist turning it on each day. When friends are over, keep the computer and TV off—at least for the first hour or two. Do homework, bake muffins, take a walk, or play a board game together. You can hardly blame a friend for being offended if you ask her over and then shut her out. Can you tell yourself you won't turn on the TV or computer until a particular hour? Can you reward yourself for trying to break what is indeed an addictive habit? When your hand goes for the button, can you turn around and do something else instead—at least sometimes? Answer: Yes, you can! P. S. You're not alone. Lots of people—grown-ups included—spend too much time staring at screens.

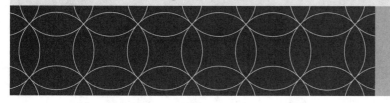

Dear Carol,

I always put off doing my homework, reports, chores, and anything else I don't really want to do. The day before a report is due, I'm up until around one in the morning getting it done. Even when I open my books as soon as I get home from school, I get sidetracked and end up doing something else, like watching TV. I want to stop procrastinating. Please tell me how.

—Last-Minute Girl

Dear L.M.G.,

You get a gold star for being aware of and wanting to change your ways. Most people procrastinate a little, but since you think you're taking things too far, you need to set some rules. Give yourself a bedtime curfew and a midweek TV limit and then reward yourself when you stick to it. Can you persuade your folks to offer you a special treat if you do go to bed earlier all week? Also, think about this: If you get your homework done before watching TV, you can enjoy watching your favorite shows guilt-free. If you get your book report done ahead of time, you'll feel light as air the week that it's due. As for better study habits, when you have to tackle a big report, do a little bit every day so the project feels manageable instead of intimidating. Setting goals for yourself and feeling proud of accomplishing them beats running out of time and feeling frantic and exhausted.

Dear Carol,

My birthday was almost three months ago and I was so busy I didn't send thank-you notes. Should I write everyone now or should I just forget about it?

—Didn't Do It

Dear Didn't Do It,

I hope you're not expecting me to let you off the hook, because I'm a big believer in written thank-yous. It's usually best (and easiest) to whip 'em off as soon as possible, but "better late than never" still applies—especially if you're hoping your friends and relatives don't forget your future birthdays! Just dash off notes that begin with a line of apology about your tardiness and then move on to a paragraph about how much the gift means to you. You can do it! In fact, you'll feel lighter and less guilty once those thank-yous are mailed.

Knowing what to do about bad or scary feelings

Dear Carol,

I have a best friend who's pretty, but overweight. She thinks she's ugly and always tells me how pretty I am. I guess it's true, but I don't want her to feel bad when she's around me. Help!

—Feeling Bad

Dear Feeling,

Do you feel bad when you're with a girl who is a better student or more athletic than you? Or when you're with a pal whose parents have a nicer car or plusher carpets? I hope not! The world is full of all sorts. If you're pretty, lucky you. Don't spend all your time being aware of your beauty, but don't feel guilty about your looks, either. Boost your friend's self-esteem by complimenting her on whatever her strong suits are: "You are so funny!" "How'd you get to be so good with animals?" "When did you learn to play the piano so well?" "You always know how to cheer me up!" Just be her friend. If you're not fixated on your looks or on hers, she probably won't be, either.

Dear Carol,

My family and I are going on vacation, and I don't want to go. I'm scared to fly after what happened on September 11, 2001.

—Nervous

Dear Nervous,

I understand your nervousness, but it's important to overcome those fears and live your life. Don't forgo your summer plans or stay home when you can go places. Plan ahead, and pack your carry-on bag with magazines, books, music, a diary, sketchpad, stationery, snacks, and a favorite stuffed animal! Keep yourself busy, and think happy, positive thoughts. Remember, too, that while everything comes with risks, statistically, air travel is still supersafe—and much safer than car travel. Will you love the flight? Maybe not. But you *will* love your vacation.

Dear Carol,

I tend to scare myself when it's dark. Like, if I have to get something from my bedroom, I think, "What if someone under the bed is waiting to grab my ankles?" Will this go on forever?

—Shaky

Dear Shaky,

I remember running home from my next-door neighbor's house through a row of dark trees, getting more spooked with every step when I was your age. Here's the good news: It *will* stop. Inside you is a Brave You and a Scared You. Next time the Scared You rants about the bogeyman, have the Brave You say, "Cut it out. Stop inventing *Scream IV*." Carry a flashlight, whistle a tune, and don't let the Scared You run the show. Also, steer clear of frightening TV shows, movies, and news. Conquering fears is smart, but so is sensible caution. Walk briskly when outside alone, don't take shortcuts through dark or isolated places on your way home, always sit near the driver on a public bus, get a cell phone if you can, and don't hesitate to yell, "Help!" if you need to. Never, *ever* get in a stranger's car—even if the person claims to be a friend of the family. A course in self-defense can also help the Brave You feel even braver.

Dear Carol,

I don't know what's wrong with me. I am happy one minute, depressed and angry the next. I constantly snap at my friends and parents. What's this about, and how can I stop it?

—Up and Down

Dear Up and Down,

It's no fun, but mood swings aren't unusual at your age. It's important to learn how to manage your moods so you don't dump on loved ones. When you snap at them, they probably withdraw or snap back. When you're nice, they're nice back, right? So practice being civil, even when you want to throw plates or slam doors. Take kickboxing or karate so you can let off steam. And get to bed earlier—lots of people who are irritable are actually sleep-deprived. If you owe your friends or family members an apology, offer it. It's never too late, and apologies go a long way. If you're feeling really blah and consistently irritable, see your school counselor or ask your parents to make an appointment with a doctor to rule out some physical or emotional problem.

Dear Carol,

I cry at night for no reason, but I'd feel dorky talking to a school counselor.
—Help!

Dear Help!,
You'd feel dorky talking to a counselor? You're feeling miserable now! Remember that counselors have heard it all. People in helping professions would never laugh or make fun of you. They *want* to help. So stop by the counselor's office and open up to figure out what's causing your crying spells.

Dear Carol,

I'm miserable and I'm not sure why. I have a great family. I play sports, sing, have great friends, but I'm still miserable. My parents constantly tell me I should see a psychiatrist. Do you know what's wrong with me and why I'm so unhappy?
—Miss Melancholy

Dear Carol,

I often get mad or cry about embarrassing things that have happened to me. I try to forget or tell myself no one remembers, but it never works.
—Amnesia, Please

Dear Amnesia,
You are at an age when a lot of things can feel embarrassing. It's normal to feel insecure and replay past incidents. But you know what? Other kids are not dwelling on your not-so-proud moments, so you shouldn't, either. Live in the here-and-now. Sign up for the debate team, drama club, or school newspaper so you can get more caught up in today and spend less time focusing on uncomfortable situations that are a long way behind you.

Dear Miss M.,
Many girls have bouts of misery, but it's not normal to feel miserable 'round the clock. If you are bummed more often than not, you owe it to yourself to check out why. At the very least, unload your feelings on the school nurse or your school's guidance counselor—that's what they are there for! They—or your folks—can also help you find a therapist whom you can talk to. You may feel self-conscious talking about your troubles, but that beats feeling miserable all alone, don't you think?

Dear Carol,

I have really bad mood swings. They make me mad or depressed. My mom expects me to act happy and pleasant all the time, but I don't. She says I am obnoxious and rude and that I only think about myself. That's not true.

—Swing Girl

Dear Swing Girl,

It's normal to be moody sometimes, so unless your down times are frightening or long-lasting, I wouldn't worry. It's also normal to let your guard down at home after you've been at school all day. Do you stop smiling the second you walk in the front door? Recognize that if you act rude with your family, they'll likely be unpleasant right back. You don't need to act pleasant 24/7, but next time Mom says, "How was your day?" instead of giving her a snide response, say, "Fine. How was yours?" If you can act semi-civil, it might just pay off. Instead of butting horns when you feel low, take a walk, phone a friend, sketch your pet, watch a video, take a nap, bake bread, read a short story, or listen to music—you get the idea.

Dear Carol,

I get frustrated very easily. I try punching a pillow and writing in my journal, but nothing works. What should I do?

—Frustrated Wreck

Dear Frustrated,

Give yourself a break for not being perfect (nobody is), and congratulate yourself for being aware of your weak spot. Why do you get frustrated? Do you measure yourself by impossible standards? Are you insanely jealous? Do you have a hopeless crush? Figure out if something specific is frustrating you and, if so, what you can do about it. It's possible you just have extra passion, drive, or anxiety, and it may help if you take up a sport to let off pent-up energy. Or start painting or playing an instrument to channel your feelings into music or art. Get enough sleep and eat healthfully so you don't lose it just because you're tired or hungry. Speak your mind instead of bottling things up. And be sure to give yourself credit for the many things that you do well.

Dear Carol,

Two of my friends occasionally experiment with cigarettes and alcohol. I don't do what they do. We're really close, and it breaks my heart to see the choices they make. Can I stay friends with them, or do I need to dump them?

—Totally Confused

Dear Confused,

I'm glad you're showing good judgment and not taking risks that could mess up your health and your life. That said, you might not need to totally break things off with your friends. Have you told them how you feel about smoking and drinking? Do they respect your attitude? I hope so. If you want to stay friends with them, why not suggest doing stuff you *all* enjoy like going to the mall or earning money by raking leaves? Make some other friends, too. While some teens/preteens experiment with cigarettes and alcohol, many more feel exactly the way you do. Seek them out!

Dear Carol,

A girl who has been my friend since kindergarten is starting to smoke. That makes me worry, but what scares me most is that she might tell me to try it. I hate cigarettes, but I don't know what to say.

—Saying No

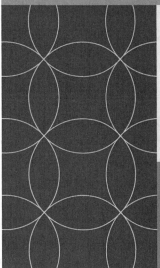

Dear Saying No,

You're right to worry about your friend. The easiest thing to say is, "Smoke gives me a headache." You could tell her that smoking makes her clothes smell bad, can turn her teeth yellow, and causes cancer. But it's OK to skip the sermon. The main thing is to take care of your own health by not smoking.

Dear Carol,

I had my cat for seven years, and she just died. I'm sad all the time. None of my friends have cats, so no one understands. My friends are starting to not like me. Mom is sad, too, but she never talks about it.

—Catless

Dear Catless,

I remember how sad I was when my Siamese died a few years ago. Since your mother loved your cat, too, talk with her. Say, "I still miss our cat so much, don't you?" Having someone to talk to about painful things can help you get through them. As for your friends, some may understand, even if they don't have pets, but they may simply not know what to say. They may also wish you'd cheer up and make an effort to talk about other things. Can you try?

Dear Carol,

I just found out my best friend smokes. She acts like it's no big deal, but it is. She is only thirteen and her parents are divorced, so she visits them both. Her dad doesn't know, but her mom is the one giving her cigarettes. I don't think I can do anything about it, but I don't want to see her get hurt. She told me not to tell anyone.

—Scared

Dear Scared,

I'm glad you know how DUMB it is to smoke and what a shame it is to pick up a smelly, bad-for-you, and expensive habit. It's terrible that her mom gives her cigarettes! While you can't change people, you can tell your friend smoking is unhealthy and that she will almost definitely get hooked. Tell her that while some kids may think smoking is cool, even more kids (like you) think it's gross. Most of all, continue to avoid cigarettes yourself.

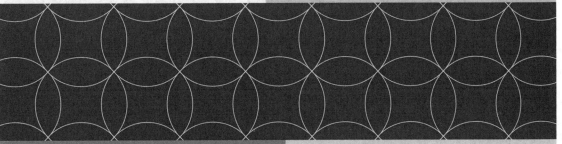

Dear Carol,

The mother of a guy in my class recently passed away. He is my friend, and I feel really bad about it because I have no idea how to talk to him without upsetting him.

—Wondering

Dear Wondering,

I'm so sorry for his loss. Don't worry about upsetting him because he is surely already upset. On the other hand, don't start talking about his mom when he's in a good mood and temporarily distracted. Just make sure he knows you're there for him when he *does* want to talk. When the two of you are alone, say, "I feel so sad for you. You must really miss your mom," or, "How are you—are things getting any easier?" Or e-mail to say that you're thinking of him. Some kids feel so awkward that they avoid friends who are in crisis, but I'm sure this boy will appreciate your efforts to continue being his friend. He lost his mom—how terrible if he were also to lose his friends!

Dear Carol,

Two days after my twelfth birthday, I shoplifted. I stole from three stores before I was caught. I felt awful, especially when my mom had to pick me up from the mall. I hate myself! How can I move on?

—Criminal at Twelve

Dear Twelve,

OK. You screwed up and you were caught. You regret it, but since you shoplifted from three stores, is it possible that deep down you wanted to get caught? Sometimes, girls who shoplift just want some attention. When they feel ignored or invisible, negative attention seems preferable to zero attention. Or maybe you were peeved with your BF or upset about getting cut from the basketball team, and felt stealing would even the score. Or maybe you were looking for an adrenaline rush—"thrill stealing." Level with yourself, and think about what made those fingers sticky. If you don't know why, you run the risk of doing it again—even if you *do* regret it. It sounds like you've learned the hard way that a "free" pair of earrings or whatever else isn't worth losing respect—for yourself and

from your parents. Instead of hating yourself, talk to your mom or a counselor about your feelings. Vow never to shoplift again, and come up with something you can do to feel proud of yourself. Helping others is a good way to regain your pride. How about visiting kids in the pediatric ward of your local hospital? Or organizing a bake sale to benefit the American Red Cross or children in need? Forgive yourself, lend a hand, and you will feel better— guaranteed.

The big life questions

Dear Carol,

I started junior high this year and I find it overwhelming.
I don't have time for all the things I love—friends, sports,
shopping. What can I do to get my life back and relax?
—Stress Mess

Dear Stress Mess,
You're not alone, and I'm sorry you're feeling stressed. Lots of hardworking
people get overwhelmed because there isn't enough time to do everything
every day. But in the grand scheme of things, there *is* enough time to do
what matters. It's just that you may have to study more during the week,
and catch up on other stuff more on weekends. This doesn't mean you
can't enjoy some daily rest and relaxation. You can! Give yourself daily
kickback time—whether that means taking a relaxing bubble bath,
e-mailing friends, reading a novel just for fun, doing yoga, listening to
music, talking on the phone, or walking your dog.

Dear Carol,
A boy I know recently died
in a fire. I realize now how
valuable life is. Should I just
go on with life? Or should I
tell everyone what I think?
—Scared of Death

Dear Scared,
Both. Go on with life and don't be afraid to tell people what you think.
This boy's tragic death probably left a mark on many others, too, so
I'm sure you're not the only person feeling sad—and yet also more
appreciative of being alive. If you know the boy's parents, write them
a letter explaining what you liked—and miss—about their son. Condolence
letters can help the writer and receiver feel a little bit better.

Dear Carol,
I don't know what I want to be when I grow up! I feel left out when friends talk about their dreams for the future.
—Unsure

Dear Unsure,
While a few lucky girls seem to know from day one that they want to be pediatricians, actors, or computer scientists, most kids need time to figure out the future. As a girl, I kept diaries, but it never occurred to me that I wanted to be a writer until I was in college. There's really no rush. Even many adults have several jobs before they discover what they most enjoy. Take your time discovering what you believe in and what you're best at. Work hard in school, sample lots of after-school activities, and find out about summer courses or camps. You may be able to volunteer at a pet shop, hospital, or at a parent's friend's business. Little by little, you'll find out which fields most appeal to you—and your future will become clearer.

Dear Carol,
I'm 13 and I've lived in the same house all my life, but now we're moving to a different part of town. I'll be going to the same school, so it's not my friends I'll miss—it's my house. It's too small for my family, but it's part of me. How can I feel better about moving?
—Attached to My House

Dear Attached,
Before you box up your belongings, why not go through your house and take pictures of every room? You can look at them if you ever feel homesick. But since you're not moving far away, maybe you won't feel as homesick as you fear. Not only can you still visit your old stomping grounds, but this is your chance to make new neighbor friends (while keeping the old) and to decorate your new room any way you want (as long as your parents approve). Your old room was for you as a kid. This one is for you as a teen. Start thinking about colors and curtains, pillows and posters. Can you buy a bulletin board and decorate it with a collage of cartoons or actors or stickers or photos? Moving is difficult, but it's also a wonderful opportunity to get organized and start fresh. Make your new house your home and you'll feel attached to it in no time.

Your Body, Yourself

Chapter 2

"Whether short, tall, curvy, or thin,
make peace with your own body."

In a perfect world, we'd all be gorgeous. But wait—what does gorgeous mean, anyway? There are many ways to look terrific, and standing tall and smiling counts for a lot.

Your goal shouldn't be to weigh a certain amount or look like a certain celebrity; it should be to be healthy and fit and to feel good about your body—no matter how quickly it is or isn't changing.

So take care of your body and start appreciating it. Think how much it does for you every single day!

Next time you look in the mirror, don't even *think* about making a face. Give yourself a smile and a thumbs-up, and, if no one's watching, go crazy and mumble a quick thank-you.

This chapter addresses some of your questions and concerns. Can't sleep? Feeling fuzzy? Ready to get in shape? Read on—but don't buy into the idea that there is only one way to be beautiful. Because you really are as beautiful as you feel!

Here's hoping you feel as gorgeous as you are!

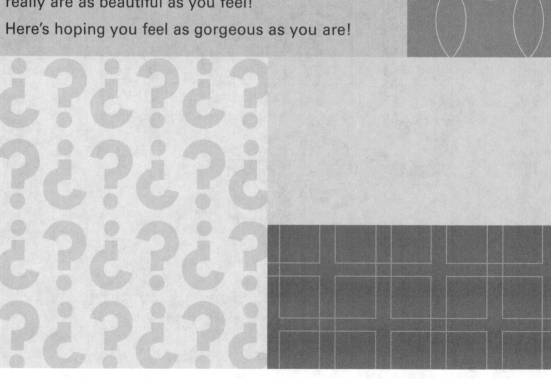

I'm so tired!

Dear Carol,

I stay up way too late every night—almost until midnight. I'm always tired and grouchy and yawning, and sometimes I even fall asleep in school. Help!
—Night Owl

Dear Night Owl,
Your body is speaking out loud and clear. It needs more sleep! Many girls are night owls, but during the school year, since you have to fly around with the early birds, you need to adjust your body's clock. Get your homework done early, turn off the TV and computer by 10 p.m., take a soothing bath, and have a glass of milk or chamomile tea. Avoid late-night cola, chocolate, spicy foods, and evening arguments. Sleep is essential and pleasurable—so don't deny yourself! Not only should you try to tuck yourself into bed earlier each night, but why not try to go to bed extra early once or twice a week? And catch extra zzz's on weekends. Napping on Saturday afternoon or sleeping in on Sunday—what could be better, or better for you?

Dear Carol,

I wake up in the middle of the night and can't get back to sleep for hours. Because of this, I am always tired.
—Sleepless

Dear Sleepless,
Is something bothering you and making you lose sleep? If you have worries, discuss them with your parents, teacher, or counselor, rather than bottling them up. Next time you feel sleepless, picture yourself floating and try not to be anxious. Tell yourself that resting counts, too. Exercise in the afternoon so you'll be good and tired, but don't work out at night because that gets your adrenaline going. Spend the hour before bed chilling out with a magazine or petting your cat. Try to have a regular bedtime so that you'll be in bed for around nine hours each night. What else? Be sure your room is quiet and dark. And if you wake up and can't sleep, don't turn on the TV. Just read until your eyes get heavy—but pick something soothing or even a bit dull—not a murder mystery!

The tall and short of it

Dear Carol,
I'm short, real short. And I'm not growing! Help!
—Simply Short

Dear Simply Short,
OK, I'm coming clean. I'm not just an advice columnist. I'm a real, live short person. In middle-school, I was obsessed with my size. I wanted to be tall, and it just didn't happen. When kids lined up by height, I was always at the short end. But one day, I looked in the mirror and said, "You're 5'2", eyes of blue. Get used to it—because you're not getting any taller." Whether short, tall, curvy, or thin, make peace with your own body. It may feel as if you are way behind or ahead of the pack, but if you look around, you'll see you are not "the only one." And besides, what's wrong with being short, hmmm?

Dear Carol,
I'm too tall and look older than I am. The guys in my class are all much shorter than I am!
—Too Tall

Dear Too Tall,
You're not too tall, you're fine just the way you are. Work on accepting your height because you can't change it. Everyone grows at their own pace. Eventually, short girls stretch a few inches, and tall girls stop growing. I know it's hard when girls and guys grow at such different rates, but just hang in there! Most of the boys will catch up soon enough. Puberty requires patience.

When the fur flies...

Dear Carol,

I want to ask my mom about shaving my legs, but I'm afraid she'll say no or get mad or laugh. Every girl I know shaves, and I feel uncomfortable having hairy legs. What should I do?

—Hairy One

Dear Hairy One,

I am certain you're not the only girl who doesn't shave, but sure, why not ask your mom? Ask in a note, e-mail, over the phone, or in person. Say, "Mom, I feel funny talking to you about this, but I want to shave my legs. A lot of girls in my grade shave, and I feel ready. Please don't get mad or laugh because I want to be able to talk to you about other girl stuff, too." If she says no, try again in a few months.

Dear Carol,

I'm twelve and very furry. My fingers, my nose, even my ears have dark hair! If I didn't secretly pluck my eyebrows, I'd have a unibrow. I'm uncomfortable in tankinis or tiny tops because my stomach hair shows. My mom won't let me bleach it, and I don't know what to do.

—Hairy Mess

Dear Hairy,

We're mammals, so we all have fuzz—even on our ears and fingers. I doubt yours is as noticeable as you think. As for feeling uncomfortable in certain clothes, many girls do—whether it's because of hair, weight, or just self-consciousness. Remind yourself what you like most about your body and choose clothes you feel good in. If the hair continues to bug you, ask your mom again about bleaching, waxing, or other options.

Tough body stuff

Dear Carol,

I'm twelve and have a male doctor. When I go for a check-up, I feel uncomfortable. I know it's his job to examine me, but I dread going to him. He's friends with my parents, so I can't casually go to a different doctor.

—Embarrassed

Dear Embarrassed,

If you told me your doctor winks at you and says, "Hubba hubba!" I would say his behavior is inappropriate and you should change doctors. But it sounds as though your doctor conducts himself professionally, and you're embarrassed because, well, checkups have their awkward moments. That's natural. You may want to switch to a female doctor, but even if you do switch, it can still feel a little uncomfortable when she asks about your body, or touches you here and there. When you feel anxious, remember that the doctor is doing his or her job. To combat embarrassed feelings, try spelling your neighbors' last names backward to distract yourself. And think about how you'll feel when you leave, knowing you're in great health.

Dear Carol,

I'm afraid that I have bad breath so I don't like to sit near boys or dance with them or anything. I worry about it a lot.

—Halitosis

Dear Halitosis,

Why would you have bad breath? More people worry about bad breath than actually have it. Brush your teeth (and even tongue) with toothpaste morning and night, and avoid garlic, onions, and other spicy foods. Ask your mom or sibling if you need to use mouthwash—they'll be honest. And carry breath mints if it will make you feel more confident. Your dentist can help if you really have a problem, but I bet you've been watching too many TV commercials. Commercials specialize in getting everybody paranoid about all sorts of things so that we'll want to spend our hard-earned money on mouthwash and other nonessential products. Think about it.

Dear Carol,

I have diabetes and I don't want my friends to know. But they already think I'm strange because I don't eat candy or dessert. I just don't know whether to tell them that I have diabetes. What do you think?

—Secret-Keeper

Dear Secret-Keeper,

Here's what matters in a friend: Warmth, intelligence, sense of humor, and good attitude. Here's what doesn't matter: Whether the person has diabetes, freckles, big feet, or a chipped tooth. How about you? If you found out your best friend had asthma, would you drop her? No. But you'd probably ask a million questions. Before you go public, talk to your doctor and parents, and find out everything you can about diabetes. If you think diabetes is weird, strange, scary, or embarrassing, your friends might, too. But if you accept yourself, your friends will, too. When you're ready, and someone tries to push a piece of chocolate on you, go ahead and tell them how you take care of yourself.

Dear Carol,

I'm allergic to peanuts, but my friend thinks I'm making it up.

—Allergic

Dear Allergic,

Many people have food allergies. Some people with extreme allergies can have a severe reaction and get immediately sick from eating something they shouldn't. So be careful! If you're lucky, you'll outgrow your allergy—many kids do. Meanwhile, explain to your friend that you *really* have to avoid peanuts, even in Halloween candy and baked goods. By the way, I heard about a girl with a peanut allergy who kissed a boy who had eaten PB&J, and she had to be rushed to the hospital! Traumatic for the girl and the guy! People with food allergies really *do* have to be on guard!

Learning to love your body

Dear Carol,

I can never find a swimsuit because I look terrible in everything. The hanging-out-in-a-tiny-bikini-for-three-months thing bums me out.

—Bathing Suit Bummed

Dear Bathing Suit Bummed,
Many people, including guys, feel the same way. Even models often confess they don't feel as radiant as they appear. Hardly anyone has a perfect bathing suit body. Try to eat right, stay active, and hold your head high. The more confident you are, the better you'll look. So act confident— even if you have to fake it at first. And don't forget the sunscreen!

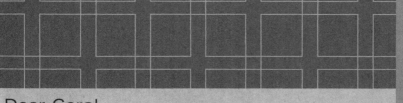

Dear Carol,

I'm thirteen, and I'm "pleasantly plump."
Is there any way to lose weight at my age,
or should I just forget about having a life?

—P.P.

Dear P.P.,
At any age, the safest and surest way to lose weight is to eat healthfully, exercise regularly, and avoid sodas and junky snacks. But wait—what does that have to do with having a life? You *have* a life! So you're "plump"—what else describes you? Fun-loving? Hardworking? Intelligent? Thoughtful? Funny? Creative? Organized? You're more than your measurements! Look around, there are plenty of happy, successful, and pleasantly plump TV stars, teachers, and students. Bottom line: It's sensible to be physically fit, but it's also sensible to stay busy and feel good about who you are—and how you look.

Dear Carol,

I am not skinny and I am not fat, but I constantly weigh myself. My friends think I do it too much. Is constantly weighing yourself bad? What do you think?

—Not Sure

Dear Not Sure,

Constantly weighing yourself *is* a bad habit. It means you're overly concerned with how much you weigh and also that you're keeping track of yourself by numbers, not by what you learned, how much fun you had, or whether you excelled at something or helped someone. Weight is a complicated subject, but since you asked, I do think scales can sometimes do more harm than good. (I don't even own a scale!) To look more fit, exercise more, and cut out soda, chips, and cookies. It's easy to snack while watching TV, but it's better to take walks, go skating, biking, sledding, or skiing. In other words, keep moving—just not to and from the scale.

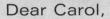

Dear Carol,

I look fat. But I am just big-boned, I think. Seven people have called me fat. Every time this happens, I cry in the bathroom stalls. Please help.

—Feeling Fat

Dear Feeling Fat,

Rude jerks! Here's my admittingly hard-to-follow advice: Try not to let those goons get you down. Don't give them any power over you. If you're comfortable with yourself, that counts a gazillion times more than the opinions of some insensitive kids. Since you're confused about how you look, find out from your doctor if you are within the normal weight range for your height. If you are, stop sweating it. If not, get some advice on how to be more fit, because being overweight is not just socially difficult, it's unhealthy.

Dear Carol,

All my friends are concerned about their weight—they are on diets and even lift weights. The thing is, they are not fat. Should I lift weights and diet like my friends? I think I look OK.

—Confused

Dear Confused,

Three cheers for not obsessing over your changing body. While some girls are truly overweight and should be commended for trying to take care of themselves, too many others are fit and fine, but become compulsive about inches and pounds. Yes, you want to look and feel good, but it's a brain drain to spend too much time counting calories. Some diets are downright dangerous. Avoid junk food and double desserts—but avoid fad diets, too. Exercising in moderation is sensible—basketball, tennis, school sports. Still interested in learning more about weight lifting? Talk to your gym teacher or coach.

Dear Carol,

I'm miserable. Lots of kids make fun of my weight. I weigh 127 pounds and I'm not tall. I know I need to lose weight, but I can't.

—Miserable

Dear Miserable,

I'm sorry those insecure kids are so thoughtless. How do I know they're insecure? Because confident kids do not get their kicks by putting others down. As for your weight, if you've always been heavy, or if your parents are also heavy, it's possible that you may always be bigger than other girls …and that's OK. In fact, accepting your own shape is a worthy goal. On the other hand, while genetics play a part, so does behavior. You say you can't lose weight, but I bet you can. The trick is to exercise and eat right—to be sure that you aren't consuming more calories than you are burning off. Can you ask your parents to buy more carrots and less cookies? If it isn't within reach, it won't tempt you. Guzzle water instead of soda. Drinking lots of water is good for you and will help slim you down. And try my S rule: Cut back on Soda, Snacks, Sweets, and Seconds. But keep active, too: Swim, hike, play a sport, work out, or just walk. You only have one body, and it's up to you to keep it in good shape. So take care of yourself, one day at a time. Want more help? Talk to your doctor or a nutritionist about setting up a smart diet and exercise program. Make this your turnaround year.

Friendship Ups and Downs

Chapter 3

"Step one to having friends
is being friendly."

Girlfriends! Where would we all be without them? Sharing popcorn and secrets, going to slumber parties, talking about music and sports, cute guys and scary movies, nail polish and clothes, books and TV, homework and...

Some of your current friends will be your friends forever. You'll call and visit for years to come, and maybe even go to one another's weddings.

Other friends are great as teammates or classmates— but not soulmates. They are buddies for now, but not necessarily for the long haul, and that's OK, too.

And a few so-called friends are, well, trouble. These girls bring you down instead of building you up. They latch onto you and won't let go. They're not caring and supportive —they're gossipy, backstabbing, or on-again-off-again.

I'm all for female bonding. But it's important to know which friends are the keepers. And which aren't.

If you're the new girl in school, or just looking to make new friends, there are ways to do that, too.

This chapter is about making and keeping good friends, and also about drifting away from not-so-good ones.

Making friends

Dear Carol,

I'm going into sixth grade, and I have no friends. I wish I had just one good friend. What am I doing wrong?

—Friendless

Dear Friendless,
You're not the only one who feels this way, and I doubt you're doing anything wrong. It takes courage, but step one to having friends is being friendly. Join an activity—theater, yearbook, science club, student council, computer club, soccer, ballet—maybe even an activity outside of school. Then, when you're next to someone, say, "Hi!" and introduce yourself. Or start up a conversation. "I liked the Greek myth we studied today, did you?" or, "I love your sweater. It looks great on you." (Questions and compliments go a long way!) Tight cliques are hard to break into, but are there any new kids in your grade who could use some new friends, too? And which other nice, yet undiscovered, girls might be fun to get to know? Who, like you, are the other hidden gems in your school? Can you say hi, chat online, and eventually invite someone over? Finally, confide in your mom, and see if she's willing to take you shopping or get you a cute new haircut so that you can begin to feel more confident about coming out of your shell.

Dear Carol,

I just moved to a school I always made fun of because I thought the kids were all snobs. My mom wants me to make new friends, but I want my old friends! I hate change, and I miss my old house and neighborhood.
—Moving Moper

Dear M.M.,

Change is hard, but it's often for the best. You made friends in your old neighborhood, and you'll make friends again. Be warm and open, and chances are your new class-mates will do the same. Find out if there are other new kids, because they'll be looking for friends, too. And sign up for chorus or band, or write for the newspaper. Resist any temptation to talk about how your old school was cooler or how you used to make fun of this school. As for keeping old friends, you can! Phone, write, e-mail, and plan visits.

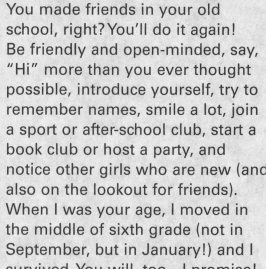

Dear Carol,

I'm starting a new school this year. How will I ever make friends?
—Worried over School

Dear Worried,

You made friends in your old school, right? You'll do it again! Be friendly and open-minded, say, "Hi" more than you ever thought possible, introduce yourself, try to remember names, smile a lot, join a sport or after-school club, start a book club or host a party, and notice other girls who are new (and also on the lookout for friends). When I was your age, I moved in the middle of sixth grade (not in September, but in January!) and I survived. You will, too—I promise!

Bud boredom busters

Dear Carol,

My best friend and I have sleepovers almost every weekend. It's always the same—popcorn and a scary movie. It's getting a little boring. How do you suggest we spice up our weekends?

—Sleepy Sleepover

Dear Sleepy,
Give each other makeovers, take magazine quizzes, bake cupcakes, pencil each other's portraits, write a song, interview each other on video, put together a scrapbook, tell ghost stories, look for constellations in the night sky, have a fashion show, do a 500-piece puzzle, play a board game, make pizza from scratch, plan a party, dance to new music, or invite some other pals over. Just not all on the same night!

Dear Carol,
Whenever my friend comes over, she doesn't like doing anything. I like her, but I'm always bored.
—She's a Boring Bud

Dear She's a Boring Bud,
Generate a good list of stuff you like to do—alone and with other friends. Get creative and add everything from playing board games by the fire, making a collage for your bulletin board, designing clothes, or taking the dog on a long walk. Instead of asking her, "What do you want to do?" and getting a shoulder shrug—be specific. Throw out your favorite suggestions, "Let's make homemade taffy, I have this awesome recipe!" Or list your three favorites and choose what to do together. Maybe she hates making decisions. Maybe she hates being put on the spot. If you make it easy for her, she might jump right in. If she's not interested in your ideas and doesn't offer her own, it doesn't mean she's a bad friend. But think twice before inviting her over next time. She might be a better lunch buddy, phone friend, or math partner, than an after-school pal. Which other friends can you invite over?

Dear Carol,
My friend comes home from school with me often, and after we do our homework, we never know what to do next—besides watch TV. Any ideas?
—Bored

Dear Bored,
How about baking an extended gingerbread family—gingerbread men, women, kids, puppies? Or be brave and try to make dinner. Or forget the kitchen and put together a bulletin board with cutouts from magazines. Paint watercolor pictures of the great outdoors, or sketch your pet or stuffed animal. Do a big puzzle. Get rid of a third of the stuff in your closet— with the promise that you'll tackle your friend's closet at her house next time. Teach each other card tricks. Write love letters that you'd NEVER send, or birthday cards that you would. Start organizing a book sale, lemonade stand, or mini crafts fair. Or just get some exercise—walking, running, skating, or biking. Down time is okay, but your friendship will grow if you don't spend all your spare time glued to the tube.

Sticky friend situations

Dear Carol,

I like my friends and I think they like me, but they always come to my house and I never go to theirs. It could be because we have a pool. What do you think?

—Confused

Dear Confused

If we were friends, I'd rather hang out in your pool than my apartment, too! Go ahead and tell your friends that you'd like to spend an afternoon at their homes or at the movies or mall, but if you all seem to be having fun together, try not to keep tabs on whose turn it is to go to whose house. In other words, if these girls visit only on scorching days and walk by you on rainy ones, then yes, something's wrong. But if you are lucky enough to have nice friends *and* a cool pool, then hey, don't second-guess a good thing. Everyone feels insecure at times. But if your friends didn't like you, they wouldn't hang out with you—pool or no pool.

Dear Carol,

My friend is a troublemaker. She'll go to my other friend's house and talk about me, and then she'll run home and call and tell me what my other friend just said about me. She must want to be friends with both of us. But she doesn't want me and my other friend to be friends. I hope you understand.

—Big Problems

Dear Big Problems,

I do. What to do now? Try honesty. Tell each girl, "Look, I really like you and I like our other friend, too. But all this gossiping is just bringing us all down, don't you think?" Here's the thing: Friends of all ages *do* talk about one another, but for the most part, they don't report all that gossip back and forth. When someone confides in you, don't turn around and tell all, irresistible as that can seem. Start talking about other stuff with your friends—that makes a better foundation for friendship, anyway.

Dear Carol,

My best friend has a friend from another school who goes to our school now. This girl always has to be right next to my best friend, and she shoves people out of the way to get there. She follows my friend everywhere and hardly lets anyone else talk to her. What can I do?

—Frustrated

Dear Frustrated,

Instead of fighting over your best friend, try being nice to this new girl, too. She's sitting to the right of your best bud? Fine, sit to the left and ask *both* of them about their weekend, or whether they read the chapter for English. Once the new girl stops feeling so dependent on your best friend, she'll probably be less possessive—and more fun to be with. Meanwhile, you can always phone your friend and make after-school plans. And spend time with others, too.

Dear Carol,

I had a best friend for three years, but then she dumped me for the popular group. It really hurt, but I made other friends. Now suddenly my ex-best friend has been calling and acting friendly again. I don't know if I can trust her, and I can't leave my new friends.

—Confused

Dear Confused,

The fact that your old friend is acting warm again (big of her!) is no reason to leave your new friends high and dry. Just because she's an unreliable friend doesn't mean *you* should be. Give your former friend a second chance, if you like, but don't ditch your new friends. It's ideal to have more than one friend, anyway.

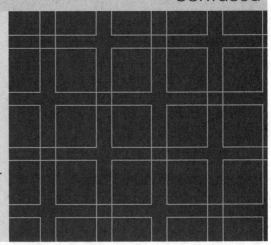

Dear Carol,

My friend wears the same clothes over and over. How can I nicely tell her she might want to change her clothes?
—One Outfit Friend

Dear One Outfit Friend,
You could suggest a little shopping trip to the mall. Or you could hold up one of your shirts to her and say, "You look great in red! You should wear more bright colors!" Or even, "Ugh, I get so tired of my clothes sometimes, don't you?" If she's smaller, or you two are the same size, hand her a bag of clothes you've outgrown or clothes you're tired of and say, "I *loved* this shirt. I'm so bummed that I outgrew it. But I thought you might like it." OK, I've answered your question. But, now I have two for you: Are you sure she can afford new clothes? And why are you so worried about what she wears, anyway?

Dear Carol,

My friends are having a fight. They are both asking me to be on their sides. My mom says to stay out of it, but I still hang out with both of them. What should I do?
—Confused

Dear Confused,
Stay out of it. If you feel you need to say something, tell your friends—separately or together—you don't want to get involved because you like them both. You can even add that you hope they'll make up.

Dear Carol,

My BFF has majorly bad body odor. How can I tell her without hurting her feelings?
—Slave to Smelling Bad B.O.

Dear Slave to Smelling,
That can be tricky. You could say nothing. Or you could say, "Look, it's because I care about you that I'm mentioning this. You should use deodorant. I do." You could also be less direct. In the locker room or next time she's over, say, "Try this and see if you like it as much as I do." Or tell her about a kid at camp who had B.O. until she finally started showering and washing her clothes more, and using deodorant. Maybe she'll get the hint, hint, hint.

Argh! She's driving me crazy

Dear Carol,

My friend isn't really acting like a friend. She's being a snot and putting boys before her friends. How can I let her know this is bugging me big-time?

—Hurt

Dear Hurt,

Try to understand that she's probably going through a boy-craze phase. You two might be temporarily out of sync, but don't give up on her— you're both still changing. Can you try to plan something the two of you would have fun doing together—decorating your jeans, baking pies, figuring out crossword puzzles, or planting a flower garden? If she comes around, great! If not, be patient, and get to know other girls in the meantime. Eventually, she might realize she's missing out and that real friendships are more rewarding than fleeting flirtations. And if you're careful with your wording, you can even try, "Hey, I like guys, too, but I still like doing things, just you and me sometimes."

Dear Carol,

I'm taking an art class with one of my buds, and she always gives me—and everyone else—pointers. When our teacher starts talking about my paintings, my friend stops what she's doing and joins in on the critiquing. I'm sick of it! How can I tell her to mind her own business?

—Frustrated Artist

Dear Frustrated,

Make eye contact and say, "I like you and your art—but I don't like it when you critique my work." Awkward? Yes. But she's speaking up, so why shouldn't you? It may also help to talk to the teacher. And remember that if your bud really believed she was up there with Picasso, she wouldn't work to keep you down. Finally, stay focused on your own projects, no matter how distracting your friend acts.

Dear Carol,

I have a friend who is a big blabber-mouth. I told her a huge secret about another friend of ours, and she told everyone, and now that other friend isn't talking to me.

—Blabber

Dear Blabber,

Sounds like you're mad at the blabber and at yourself. If you couldn't keep your mouth shut, it's a lot to expect someone else to do so. Obviously you shouldn't tell the blabbermouth any more secrets. Maybe someday she'll learn to be more discreet, but the fact is, lots of kids and adults can't resist sharing other people's juicy gossip. So keep secrets to yourself or, at least, don't confide in someone who has a bad track record for going public with what should stay private. If you just have to let a secret out, write it instead of telling it. Keeping a diary is fun and makes memories last forever. As for your understandably angry friend, if I were you, I'd apologize. Not a lame, "I'm sorry if you're mad." But a genuine, "I'm really sorry that I was such an idiot. I've learned to keep my mouth shut, and I hope you'll forgive me, though you have a right to be mad."

Dear Carol,

I have a friend who always copies me. The other day I got a T-shirt for my soccer team to sign, and then she did the same thing. (She's on my team, too.) I don't like it.

—Mad

Dear Mad,
They say imitation is the highest form of flattery. When she copies you, say, "I'm glad you liked my idea." Try to think of it as a compliment instead of an injustice. Keep complimenting her on her own ideas, too. And know deep down that you are a creative independent thinker—and that others near you know this as well.

Dear Carol,

Christin is my best friend, and Anna is my second best friend. Anna and I were in the same class last year, but we got separated this year. Now she's jealous because Christin and I hang out a lot. It's like Anna is competing for me or something.

—Frustrated

Dear Frustrated,
It's hard when friends are possessive or competitive. As Anna gets closer with the girls in her own class, she'll probably start worrying less about you and Christin. In the meantime, reassure her that you still care about her. Call her after school. Invite her to go skating or to watch videos. Arrange a sleepover. Or just tell her that although you two don't get to sit together in class anymore, you still consider her a really good friend— now and always. (After all, wouldn't *you* feel a smidge left out next year if Christin and Anna hung out all the time and forgot to sometimes call or include you?)

Dear Carol,

I had a sleepover and invited an older friend, but the rest were my age. I thought I would be the star of the party, but my older friend was. It was horrible. No one wanted to talk to me. They all wanted to talk to her.

—Broken Heart

Dear Broken Heart,

Bummer! But wait. Horrible? You gave a party at which your friends all got along. You were the hostess with the mostest. You invited a friend whom everyone liked. Your friends had fun, thanks to *you*. Maybe that's not so horrible. Horrible is giving a party and nobody showing up—or everybody yawning all night. I'm sorry you felt upstaged, and I know attention can be nice. But just because your friends liked the older girl doesn't mean they no longer appreciate you. You wouldn't want them to have ignored your older friend, right? As long as your friends like you, it's all right if they also like other people, too. (Also, sometimes a new person is temporarily more interesting.) Next time you're feeling overlooked (or brokenhearted), try joining a conversation instead of just waiting for others to talk to you. And keep throwing parties!

Bigger friendship problems

Dear Carol,

My friend is too aggressive. She always slaps me on my arm or head—and she's strong! Sometimes, I wish I'd never met her. I like being her friend, but not when she treats me like that. I don't know how to make her stop.

—Annoyed

Dear Annoyed,

What do you mean you don't know how to make her stop? If you say, "I like you, but I don't like when you hit me," you'll be doing *both* of you a big favor. If you can't seem to talk to her or she won't change, keep your distance and make some new, kinder (and gentler) friends.

Dear Carol,

I have two best friends, but we all talk behind each other's backs. One day, I got mad at one friend and talked about her to my other friend. Then my other friend got on the phone and talked about me, and then we all talked about how stupid the other one was. Now we're all so mad, I'm not sure we're really friends anymore.

—Untrusted

Dear Untrusted,

Lots of people talk about one another, but you have to be discreet about it. No good ever comes from a sentence that begins, "Don't tell her I told you..." If, despite all the gossip, you three are still getting along, then yes, you are friends. Just make a serious effort to stop talking about each other behind closed doors. Friends support and encourage one another; they don't bring each other down. Fortunately, you really want things to change for the better—so set the good example. You can even say, "Hey, I miss you and I'm sorry for what I said. I want to start over and have us not be critical of each other. We're friends—not enemies!" Threesomes are harder than twosomes, but there is enough of each of you to go around—there's no need to worry that you can't all be friends, because you can.

Dear Carol,

My best friend always brags. She brags about her blond hair, grades, and cheerleading. Enough already!
—The Non-bragger

Dear Non-bragger,

Sometimes people brag to cover up insecurities. When you feel great about yourself, you don't have to work hard to convince others how amazing you are. Of course, some crowing is OK. It's ideal when friends can tell each other their triumphs and setbacks. But when friends brag, that's a different story. Since you call this girl your best friend, let her know you cherish her and think she's terrific, but you wish she wouldn't brag so much. Tell her you like everything else about her—if you really do.

Dear Carol,

One of my friends lies all the time. No joke. She always makes up stories about her sister and brother (if she even has any). One time I called her house, and she pretended to be her sister. I knew it was her, and she finally 'fessed up. How can I tell her to stop making up stories?

—Show's Over, Sister

Dear S.O.S.,

Your friend's probably exercising her vivid imagination because she wishes she had more siblings and adventures. In person or in a note, tell her you like her best when she's honest with you. Can't be that direct? Tell her people who make stuff up are hard to trust, and that you like sincere people who tell the truth. Maybe she'll get the hint. Since she is probably insecure, try building her up by praising the qualities you like in her. If she doesn't change her ways, decide whether to accept her as is or hang out with more trustworthy buds.

Dear Carol,

My best friend has low self-esteem. She always puts herself down and compliments me. I really like her but it gets annoying and I don't know how to help. Her parents are divorced, and she always fights with her mom.

—BF Prob

Dear BF Prob,

Think of three things you like about your best friend. Now tell them to her, adding that the only thing you don't like about her is that she's constantly belittling herself. Tell her it's a bad habit. It's too bad she and her mom are at odds—parents don't always do all they can to boost kids' egos and help kids feel wanted and wonderful. Encourage your mom to invite your friend for dinner, and ask your mom to offer some encouragement of her own. Finally, tell your friend that we all have little gnomes on our shoulders—one is kind, one is nasty. My nice gnome whispers that I'm positively brilliant. My nasty one sneers that I'm a moron. So I tune out the criticism and turn up the volume on the praise. We should all do the best we can and listen to the good gnomes who are saying, "Way to go!" That's *my* secret to self-confidence. Feel free to pass it on.

feeling left out

Dear Carol,

Help! My best friend is getting sick of me. She and two other girls keep sitting next to one another, and I feel left out. I feel like I'm acting like her shadow because I always want to be next to her.

—Shadow

Dear Shadow,

It's hard when friendships shift, but you may have to give her a little space and try to make plans with other girls. Do you have any friends you haven't seen in a while? Call them up. Make an effort to meet new friends, including anyone new in town. Join a new activity. You may even find that as you step away from your old friend, you'll actually become closer again. Right now, as it stands, this rapport isn't fun for either of you. She probably feels smothered and you feel too needy. So you're smart to recognize that you need to take a deep breath and back off a little. Get out there and start complimenting, talking to, and hanging out with other girls.

Dear Carol,

This girl who used to be my friend just invited the entire class to her birthday party except me and one other girl. I don't have the guts to say anything.

—Hurt

Dear Hurt,

That's awful. I'm sorry! You *could* talk to your one-time friend in private and tell her how you feel and say that you miss your old friendship (if you do). Or, you could just sigh and accept that friendships can shift when you least expect it. Her leaving out just two girls shows an unimpressive lack of generosity, so while I wouldn't work hard to be her enemy, she doesn't sound like ideal lifelong friendship material. Anyway, plan something fun for yourself the day of the party. Go to dinner with your mom, watch a funny movie, hang out with the other girl who wasn't invited (if you like her) or with someone in another class—or even a friend from a different school.

But I don't want to be friends!

Dear Carol,

Two girls live in my apartment building. They are older and tell me who to be. I want to tell them I don't want to be friends, but I don't want to hurt their feelings.

—Trapped

Dear Trapped,

No one gets to tell you who to be! Ever. Only you can decide that. If these girls show up and you don't want to invite them in, say, "Thanks for stopping by, but I'm busy right now." When you make yourself less available, people usually get the hint—and you're spared having to say something awkward like, "I don't want to be friends." Can you work out a code with your parents so they can help cover for you? If the phone rings or one of these girls stops by with an invitation, say, "Mom, can I go out now?" while rubbing your chin so your mom knows this is her cue to say, "Sorry, dear, you still have some chores to do."

Dear Carol,

Last summer, my best friend for nearly all my life found a new friend at camp. It wasn't so bad, at first, but she always talks about writing and calling her camp friend, and how she can't wait to see her this summer. She says it to my face! Should I tell her how I feel?

—Betrayed

Dear Betrayed,
Two of my favorite things about being an adult are that we don't mind when friends have other friends and that no one tries to rub it in. But have you really been betrayed? Your sister didn't steal your boyfriend. Your parents didn't give away your room. Your neighbor didn't post your secrets on the Internet. True, your friend made another friend, but that's not the end of the world, is it? What's bad is that she's boasting about it and that you're letting it get to you. Try to be honest with your friend and say, "Look, I know you're excited to see your camp friend, but enough already." Also, why not work harder to make your own new friends? It's never too late to say "hi" to a girl in chemistry lab or invite a new neighbor over to listen to your favorite CDs.

Tough friend stuff

Dear Carol,

I live in a small apartment above a grocery store, and it's always a mess. My father never cleans it, and my mother lives in a different state. Friends never want to come over, and I can hardly blame them. What should I do?

—Home Alone

Dear Home Alone,
Your frustration is understandable. First of all, why not take charge of straightening your own home, with or without your dad's help? Put on some music, neaten things up, throw things out, and you'll be glad you minimized the mess. But don't let your home hold you back. If friends aren't coming over, meet them at the park, pond, playground, or pizza place! Go to their homes. See a movie together. Or shop. Yes, it's pretty cool to have a big, mess-free home, but in the long run, being enthusiastic, flexible, and a good listener (in short, being friendly) will earn you true friends—in school and out.

Dear Carol,

I wear a hearing aid. My so-called BFFs make fun of me when I can't hear them. How do I deal?

—Frustrated

Dear Frustrated,

Your friends make fun of you? That's so lame! They don't sound like ideal friends. Lots of people have hearing problems—or other issues—so hang in there. These are hard years, and some (insecure) girls go through a mean phase they probably will outgrow. For now, give your close friends a lesson in sensitivity. Tell them it hurts when they diss you, and ask if they'd mind sticking up for you instead. Remind them your hearing problem isn't your fault and that you do your best to keep up with the conversation. They could help by not whispering or talking with their backs to you. Keep your eye out for new friends, too. By the way, kids who overcome obstacles often become extremely strong and empathetic adults. You will, too.

Dear Carol,

My friends and I are bullied by a girl at school. She's our age, but we can't stop her from being a total brat. She goes around giving people "fashion checks," and says stuff like, "Change those jeans. They're looking pretty ratty." I am so mad! I want to do something, but I don't know what!

—Totally Helpless

Dear Totally,

That girl is looking for attention, and you and your friends are giving it to her! Next time she makes an obnoxious comment, shrug it off the way you'd shoo away an annoying fly. Let her brattiness be *her* problem, not yours. Girls like that eventually fall on their faces, or realize making catty comments is a pathetic way to amuse themselves, and they grow out of it. Instead of telling her off, tell yourself it must stink to be so insecure that she has to put others down to build herself up. Thinking about it this way should make you feel better.

Dear Carol,

My friend is ashamed of her weight because her dad called her fat. She's actually really healthy, and her weight seems fine to me. Ever since her dad said that to her, she's been acting weird. Like at lunch, when I offered her some candy—she took the package, looked at the fat grams, and said, "No, I'm not hungry." I'm worried about her.

—Worried

Dear Worried,

If she were skeletal or throwing up after meals, I would certainly worry, too. But if she is healthy and is cutting down on her candy consumption, no biggie—in fact, she may be making smart choices. It was, however, extremely uncool of her dad to tell her she's fat. Suggest to your friend that she confront her father and nicely explain that his comment upset her. Name-calling by parents can be very destructive to kids of any age. Can you help boost her confidence? Keep telling her, "You look great," and compliment her about stuff that has nothing to do with how she looks.

Dear Carol,

My parents found out my BFF's dad hit her on a couple of occasions. Now, I'm not allowed to go over to her house. She doesn't know that I know and it's getting tough to come up with excuses. Should I tell her?

—Banned from Bonding with BFF

Dear BFBWBFF,

This is a hard one. I don't blame your parents for wanting to protect you, and I don't blame you for being loyal to your friend. First of all, I am assuming her dad's abuse is a fact, and not just an awful rumor. Nothing would be worse then going along with unfounded town gossip. So, that aside, I worry that if you come out and tell her the truth, she will be devastated. Even if the abuse happened in the past, your friend still deals with it every day. Abuse is not something most people feel comfortable "just talking" about, even with their best friends. Hopefully, she is talking with a professional and discussing her feelings with an expert. So tread lightly. At some point, she may be relieved to have a sympathetic and understanding friend to talk to about it. In the meantime, keep making an effort to see your friend at your house, parties, movies, school, and at a mutual friend's place.

Time to say good-bye?

Dear Carol,

I feel like a backup best friend. When my friends argue, they come to me. But when they make up, sometimes they won't even talk to me. That happens with about ten of my friends. Half the time I feel really lonely and left out, but as soon as there is a fight, I get a friend. Please help me. My parents said to get new friends. But I don't want new friends. It took me five years to get the ones I have.

—Backup

Dear Backup,
Just because you don't have one particular best friend doesn't mean you are a second-class citizen. If you like many girls and many like you, that's not all bad. But are you waiting around for them to argue? Try taking a more active role in your social life. How about inviting a girl over to hang out or do homework with you? If all ten girls would really say no, your parents are right—you'd be wise to find new friends. But I bet most would gladly spend more time with you, if you took the initiative. Invite them over. Maybe even to a slumber party.

Dear Carol,

I have a friend who is bossy, demanding, pushy, and powerful. I like her, but we fight a lot, and sometimes I think I hate her. How do I handle this friendship?
—Sinking Friendship

Dear Sinking Friendship,
It's good to recognize which friendships make you feel good and which drag you down. If you two can't (or don't want to) work things out, give yourselves some breathing room. Don't dump her in a dramatic way or diss her left and right. Just join an extracurricular activity that she's not in, or call and make plans with others.

Dear Carol,

My two so-called friends came over and hadn't been in my house for more than ten minutes when they asked, "Can we go in your hot tub?" I asked my mom if it was OK, and she said something I had never thought about. She asked me if they were actually my friends or if they were just using me. Then I realized it was true—they just want me for my hot tub. This makes me feel sad and lonely.

—School Is One Big Popularity Contest

Dear Contest,

School is one big popularity contest only if you buy into all that. So try not to. If these two girls are never nice to you *except* when they want to have a soak, that stinks. But if you sometimes hang out together outside of the hot tub, then it's OK if they want to hit the tub now and then. (Hot tubs are fun!) Think about all this before totally writing them off, but get to know different girls, too. Which girls can you be yourself with and laugh with and confide in? They are the keepers. Finally, think about this: Some moms worry that their kids will repeat their mistakes. Moms who were shy or overweight or bossy in school might project their former selves onto their happy, well-adjusted kids. In other words, is your mom right, or is it possible that she felt taken advantage of in school and is overly concerned that this could happen to you?

Dear Carol,

I have a friend who is really rowdy and wild. I am always mad at her because she loves to embarrass me.

—Furious

Dear Furious,

It's OK for her to be naturally rowdy, but if she gets a kick out of embarrassing you, well, that's just plain mean. Who needs a friend like that? It may be time for you to take some time apart. Be frank with her about your feelings, and if she doesn't adjust her attitude, steer clear of her by subtly spending more time with other friends. In other words, don't try to change her out-there personality, but if you don't enjoy her company, don't hang out with her, either.

Dear Carol,

Whenever I get upset, my friend says, "That's a stupid thing to cry about." It hurts, so finally, I said, "I think we should go our separate ways for a while." She got mad and said we shouldn't be friends at all. It's a mess. Did I make the right choice in letting her go for a while?
—Mess

Dear Mess,
You might have made the right decision to let her go for a while, but you could have just become quietly more distant rather than announce that the friendship was history. Perhaps it's not too late to explain to her that when you're upset, you'd prefer it if she'd say something comforting (like, "I'm sorry you're feeling sad") rather than critical (like, "That's a stupid thing to cry about"). If you miss her, tell her, or write her a letter. On the other hand, maybe your best bet is to get back on good terms with each other, but not really jump-start the old friendship. She doesn't sound like the most sensitive and supportive girl in the world, and in some cases, it's better for two girls to be *friendly*, but not be actual friends.

Dear Carol,

One of my friends is always worried about what I look like, how I'm dressed, or how I did my hair. I always tell her to worry about herself, but she says she doesn't need to. Everybody says she treats me like dirt, but I can't stop being her friend because we've been friends for seven years. What should I do?
—Confused

Dear Confused,
It is nice to have old friends, but it sounds as though yours is going through an annoying phase! Tell her once again that you use a mirror, thank you, and that unless she's going to compliment you, she should keep her remarks to herself because they are making you want to avoid her. She's probably hurling insults because she is insecure, so if you feel like being mature and complimenting her, go for it. But if you'd rather just keep your distance for now and get closer to others, that's fair, too. The main point is this: Let her unpleasantness be *her* problem, not yours!

Dear Carol,

I'm in fifth grade and I'm getting pretty popular. The problem is that I've been friends with a girl in my class since kindergarten, and my new friends don't like her. I still do, but she can be a little clingy. I'm thinking of telling her that I don't want to be friends anymore, but will that hurt her feelings?

—Stuck

Dear Stuck,

Yes. If you tell her you're ready to dump her after years of friendship, you will indeed hurt her feelings. There are reasons you've liked her for so long, right? And there are reasons why she's clingy—she can sense that you're pulling away. Do you really have to choose between old friends and new ones? Says who? Not me. I say you're allowed to be friends with girls from more than one group. In fact, it's a good way to go. Why not make a weekend plan with your old friend and do the things you always enjoyed together. She knows that you've got new friends and she'll probably start making some new friends, too. But there's no limit on how many friends a girl gets to have.

Dear Carol,

Every time I go online, all my e-mails are the same dumb forwarded jokes and stupid chain letters that end with, "Send this to 10 people or your crush won't like you." Do my friends really think that if we keep sending each other the same things over and over, our crushes will care one way or another? Are my friends seriously lame?

—Enough E-mail

Dear Enough E-mail,

Don't ditch your friends, but *do* tell them that you'd rather receive an original line than a joke that's gone back-and-forth fifty times. Tell them to send you only the good stuff. You'll be doing them a favor! Lots of girls and guys forward mail as a way to say hi, so your friends probably mean well. But I agree that a real hello—online or in person—is much better than the canned kind.

Boys, Boys, Boys

Chapter 4

"Always be yourself."

You know that short kid you used to feed ducks with? When did he get so tall and cute? And how come you blush whenever he smiles at you? And why is it hard to meet his eyes and then practically impossible to look away?

What's going on here?

This chapter is all about boys, the nice ones, the less nice ones, the ones you like who like you back, and the ones you haven't yet noticed but who deserve a second look...and a third!

There's no reason to rush a crush or to race into romance. But if you're curious about the male half of the world, keep reading.

Boys, who needs 'em?

Dear Carol,

Everyone in my grade is talking about going out with boys, but none of us are really allowed to go out yet.

—Don't Get It

Dear Don't Get It,

Young couples who are "going out" aren't usually going anywhere. They can't drive or go out at night, so they talk, take walks, play games, watch videos, e-mail, phone, hang out, and just get to know each other better—not so different from what girls do when they get together. Of course, with a boyfriend, there might be extra smiling or nervousness, as well as some hand-holding, or even kissing. For now, please know that, there is more talking about going out than actually going out, and most middle-school girls and guys have not paired off yet!

Dear Carol,

I have more friends who are boys than girls. My girlfriends tease me about this.

—Just Friends

Dear Just Friends,

Nothing is wrong with having friends who are boys. Could your girlfriends be envious? When people make fun of you, it's always good to ask yourself why they are doing so. On the other hand, I hope at least one of your girlfriends is someone you can really talk to. It's ideal to have close friends who are male *and* female.

Dear Carol,

There is a boy I like, but only as a friend. We sit together every day at lunch, and every day we have to put up with kids teasing us about "going together." They should concentrate on their own lives and let us eat our lunch in peace. What do you think?

—Bugged Out

Dear Bugged,

They should, but maybe they're jealous. Or maybe they feel left out since you two have lunch together every single day. Ignore their remarks or invite them to join you. It's your call.

Dear Carol,

I hate to admit it, but I'm a major flirt. I'm popular, and all of the unpopular girls envy me, but I envy them! Three of my guy friends have fallen for me. How can I make guys less interested in me? I don't even *want* a boyfriend!

—Big Flirt

Dear Big Flirt,
Flirting can be fun. Who doesn't enjoy compliments, some attention, and a little ego stroking? But flirting is also very powerful, and if you're winking at a boy who would do anything to be your guy (when you don't like him that way), it can be unfair and hurtful. Major flirting with guys you're not interested in could get you a reputation for being a tease. (Yes, guys talk about girls just as girls talk about guys.) So if you aren't interested in a guy, be friendly, not flirty. And since these three crushing guys are your friends, treat them as such, rather than sending them mixed signals. If necessary, tell them you're flattered, but not interested in going out—you want to stay friends. As for not ever wanting a boyfriend, never say never!

Dear Carol,

I want to be friends with guys. But whenever I try to start a friendship with one, people say I'm flirting. Plus, this one guy I've been talking to is *never* friendly back.

—Flirt?

Dear Flirt?,

Flirting is when you laugh extra merrily, gaze into a guy's eyes, use his name a lot, touch his arm gently, and sparkle like crazy. Talking is different—it's just talking. And I highly recommend it when you want to just be friends with boys. While some guys don't want to be friendly back (their loss!), others do. So keep striking up conversations with whomever you want, and when you cross that talking-flirting line, at least be aware of it. As for the guy who isn't friendly back, talk to him less often, or less enthusiastically.

Dear Carol,

A couple of boys always tease me. My friends say it's because they like me. Is this true?

—Teased

Dear Teased,

Sometimes boys tease girls they like. Sometimes it's because they're immature. Is the teasing affectionate (sort of funny, sort of sweet) or mean (hurts your feelings)? If it's affectionate, smile or tease back if you like the guys. If it's mean, ignore them and don't give them the power to make you feel bad!

'Cause I don't like him!

Dear Carol,

This guy thinks he's in love with me, but I hate him. What should I do?

—Clueless

Dear Clueless,

Don't be mean to the poor guy! So he has good taste. Hate is a brain drain. Can't you just ignore him? He probably already realizes his chances with you are slim, so he'll move on soon enough.

Dear Carol,

My best friend is a guy, and I have known him forever. He is my total BFF. We were hanging out in the kitchen when he tried to tickle me. I'm not ready for a boyfriend yet, especially my bud!

—Not Ready Yet

Dear Not Ready,

Tell your friend, perhaps on the phone, that you like him as a best friend, not a boyfriend, and that you don't want to date anyone yet. Tell him you don't want to lose your friendship, but you won't feel comfortable being alone with him if he acts like he wants to be romantic. For a while, you two could get together outside rather than inside. Try meeting him for in-line skating in the park instead of movies in the dark. If he doesn't respect your feelings and stop trying to tickle you, you may have to give this relationship some space.

Crushes!

Dear Carol,

What do boys look for? I don't have it.
—Invisible

Dear Invisible,

First, boys notice the superficial stuff—just as girls do. But boys also notice—and appreciate—girls who are smart, enthusiastic, thoughtful, fun, funny, or who just manage to make them feel special or comfortable. Try to talk with different guys, and don't be afraid to look up and smile. Pay attention, too, to all the "invisible" boys out there. Many of them really are great guys who deserve to be discovered.

Dear Carol,

I have a crush on this guy. What now?
—Crushful

Dear Crushful,

If he's someone else's BF, do nothing. If he's a sweet, available guy, smile and say, "Hi." If he smiles back, ask about things that interest him, like music, movies, or vacation plans. It's OK if he notices you're happy to see him—now try to figure out if he seems happy to see you, too. Should you ask him if he likes you back? No! He might not want to answer, or he might not give the answer you want. Flirting is fine, but don't rush a crush.

Dear Carol,

I secretly have a huge crush on one of my guy friends. I'm not sure about it, but I think he likes me, too. How can I be certain?
—Want to Know

Dear Want to Know,

Sorry, there are no surefire ways to decode a guy's feelings because some guys (like some girls) are outgoing, flirtatious, and charming while others are quiet, shy, and sweet. But if he spends a lot of time and energy paying attention to you, that's a positive sign! Keep talking, e-mailing, and making eye-contact, and things will probably become clearer.

Dear Carol,

I like this boy in class. I don't know if he likes me, but I want him to. I try to be myself, but it's hard. I've also tried to act unlike myself. He is really nice and always smiles at me. How should I act?

—Need Advice

Dear Need,

Always be yourself. That's better than pretending that you're way into, say, sports, and then having your crush find out you don't know Tiger Woods from Tony the Tiger! But don't just be yourself—be your *best* self. Be friendly, fun, and interesting. Compliment how he looks, his goals, or his handwriting (if it's neat!). Ask about his weekend, new pet, or math homework. Pay attention to him in a caring way. That's what he's doing with you, right?

Dear Carol,

How can I go about asking a guy out? I've liked this guy forever, but I'm scared to say, "Want to come hang out on Saturday night?"

—Ready

Dear Ready,

Sometimes, fear is your friend. Unless you and this boy are doing some serious flirting and he's giving you a bright green light, it could be risky to ask him out. You don't want to put him on the spot, and he might need time to evaluate his feelings—and whether he's willing to make them public. A safe way to ask a guy out is something like, "Will you be at Stephanie's party this weekend?" This shows him you're into him, but in a discreet way. You could also say, "Some of us are going bowling tomorrow. Want to come?" He might say, "Sure." Or he might say, "Sorry." If he declines, do not—I repeat, *do not*—say, "Then how about Saturday or Sunday or next weekend or the weekend after that?" You want to seem interested, not desperate. Oh, and make sure you've already talked to your parents about dating. It would be pretty embarrassing if your crush said, "Sure," but your parents said, "No way!"

Dear Carol,

I invited this guy from camp to a dance at my school, and he said yes. I like him more than just as a friend. How do I tell him?

—Desperate

Dear Desperate,
You asked him to a dance, and he accepted your offer. That's great, not desperate! For now, you don't have to tell him anything else. It should be obvious you like him since you asked him to the dance, so there's no need to spell it out and force him to respond. Once you're at the dance, he might realize he likes you more—or you might realize you like him less. Take things slowly, and see what happens before you make any rash declarations of your affection toward him.

Dear Carol,

My rec center just had a dance, and all the girls had a guy to dance with—except for me and the girls who didn't want to dance. I was really sad because I wanted to dance. I feel like none of the boys like me.

—Partnerless

Dear Partnerless,
Ouch...but I bet you won't stay partnerless for long. Boys get shy, especially at dances, and some of them may like you, but not want to show it publicly. Be friendly, and at the next dance, try to catch a guy's eye, share a smile, and be the one to say, "Want to dance?" (It does take guts.) By the way, my hunch is that some of the other girls who claimed they didn't want to dance may have been feeling every bit as bummed as you were.

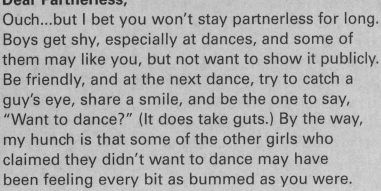

Dear Carol,

I really like this guy. He knows it, but he's not interested. I think he's perfect. How can I either get over him or get him to go out with me?

—Get Over or Go Out?

Dear Get Over,

If you've shown an interest and he's shown none (sigh), please realize he is so not perfect, because he doesn't appreciate wonderful you! Accept it. Get together with your BFF, study for that upcoming math quiz, focus on your horseback riding lessons. Say "hi" to at least two new guys this week, and get together with a group of girlfriends. While you're out having fun, you just might meet a new guy—one who *is* interested. The best crushes come when you least expect them.

Oh, boy!

Dear Carol,

I like this guy a lot, but he's thirteen and in eighth grade. I'm twelve and in sixth. He likes me, too. I've never had a BF before. Is he too old for me? Am I too young to have a BF at all?

—Preteen in Distress

Dear Preteen,

Not necessarily. But since you feel distressed, it sounds like you're not ready to have a BF. No prob! Don't talk yourself into it, if you'd rather keep things friendly. If he asks, tell him you like him, but aren't ready for a relationship. If you *do* go out with this guy, remember that it's OK to hold hands and not kiss, or kiss but only kiss. Never do things you don't want to do with a boy. After all, having a BF isn't supposed to make you feel uptight or uneasy. Just happy.

Dear Carol,

My friend has a BIG crush on this boy at school. Recently, I realized I have a small crush on him, too. I don't want to hurt her. How can I control my feelings? I'm afraid to tell anyone.

—Confused

Dear Confused,
While it's better when friends don't have crushes on the same boy, you're not breaking the law by discreetly liking a boy another girl likes. (After all, they aren't going out.) Still, crushes come and go, and friends you care about are precious and valuable. What to do? Look around to see if anyone else interests you. Is there an after-school group in which you could meet other boys? It's never a good idea to jeopardize a friendship, so proceed with caution.

Dear Carol,

There are two really cute boys at school. One sits near me sometimes, and I think he likes me. The other one, when I stare at him, says, "What are you looking at?" I think he likes another girl. Which one should I like?

—Lovebird

Dear Lovebird,
Hurray! An easy question. Let's see. You like two guys—one is nice back and one's a jerk. Well, if you want a two-way relationship that makes you feel good, pick the guy you like who likes you. If you want to invite an obsession that leaves your ego as flat as the floor, pick the one who isn't nice to you. Seriously, why choose a guy who isn't choosing you? What kind of a boyfriend would he make? Oh, and just so you know, I'm sure there are more than just two worthy guys in your school.

Dear Carol,

One of my close guy friends is going out with my BFF. I like this guy a lot as a friend, but I admit, I am jealous of their relationship. I am worried I'm losing two great friends.

—Worried, Jealous, Sad

Dear Worried,

A little jealousy is perfectly natural. But *a lot* of jealousy can poison friendships. Take a deep breath, and try to be happy for them. If you feel you need some one-on-one time with either of them, it's OK to confess your feelings. But next time you get hung up about any of this, remember that time may change your relationships anyway. So do your best to stay friends with both.

Dear Carol,

I like to chat online. Everyone in the chat rooms has e-BFs and e-GFs. Recently I've been flirting with this boy. First of all, is it safe to have an e-BF? I mean, I know all the basic rules like: Don't give your real name, address, phone number, or picture. Second, should I tell him I like him?

—Internet Crush

Dear Internet Crush,

If you don't just *know* the rules, but you stick to them, it may be safe so long as his flirty lines don't turn into gross ones. On the other hand, if you ever, ever, ever arrange to meet him, you're running a serious risk because, as I'm sure you've heard, there have been tragic cases of girls getting kidnapped, hurt, and even killed by online "sweeties." While I'm issuing warnings, let me add that a lesser danger of having an online boyfriend is that it's almost too easy. You can type in that you think about him all the time, and he can type back the same. Yet your e-romance is not reality-based. You might actually have little in common and might not be each other's type at all. In fact, he might be twice your age and have a thing for young girls. I would not tell this person (whom you don't really even know) that you like him. Even if you e-mail all the time, you don't honestly know each other. There are people out there who have mastered the art of sounding young, fun, nice, and genuine—but they're not. That's what makes the whole thing so scary. I think that falling for an online guy can spell h-e-a-r-t-a-c-h-e offline, or worse. Try to get to know some boys at school, instead.

The kiss question

Dear Carol,
I'm twelve and there's a boy I really like. At this dance, he kissed me. I loved it. Is it OK for people to kiss if they want to?
—Kiss Question

Dear Kiss,
You and this boy care about each other, so I see no crime. It's nicer to share your first kiss with a boyfriend than to kiss somebody you're not even going with. Twelve is young, though, and most girls have not had a first kiss yet—no matter what you hear in the hallway! Is it OK? Well, you don't mention that you've given up on friends or school to spend 24/7 with him. And you don't say you can't wait to get beyond kissing. So, you sound like a reasonable person with a budding romance. Please know, though, that if you break up down the road or your second kiss doesn't come for a while, that is all right, too!

Breaking up

Dear Carol,
I broke up with my crush. And only one week after I broke up with him, he got a new GF. It bothers me, even though I don't like him.
—Bothered by Breakup

Dear Bothered by Breakup,
Since you don't want to hang out with him, you really can't object that he found a girl who does. Maybe you're bothered because you don't want to think of yourself as replaceable (which you shouldn't!). Maybe you still have some feelings for him—even if you don't realize it. Or, maybe you feel a little rejected. All of these are normal feelings following a breakup— even if *you* did the breaking up. But just hang in there, and get busy with friends and projects and you'll be fine. And *pssst*, his moving on so quickly doesn't make him seem like the catch of the year, anyway.

Dear Carol,
I fake-dumped my boyfriend a few weeks ago to test his feelings for me. After that, I tried to tell him that it was a test and didn't mean anything. I asked if he would forgive me and he said no. Now he's going out with a different girl and not talking to me. What should I do? I can't take it anymore!
—Heart Broken

Dear Heart Broken,
Ouch! Poor guy! And now, poor you! I'm afraid he learned not to fully trust you and you learned (the hard way) not to play games with other people's hearts. It would have been one thing if you had played mildly hard-to-get. But since you pretend-dumped him, he may have been devastated. No wonder he doesn't want to say, "Sure, let's go back to where we were." Ask yourself if things really were perfect in paradise in the first place, and try to remember that most school relationships do end for one reason or another. Breakups hurt, but everyone survives. Make plans with girlfriends and your family, and start getting to know new guys, too. From now on, when you want to know how someone feels about you, ask him, don't trick him.

Dear Carol,
I have a boyfriend, and this is the third time we've gone out. He dumped me twice and asked me out again. I'm not sure if he likes me or if I'm just conveniently there when he wants me to be.
—Confused

Dear Confused,
I don't know if he really likes you, but do you reeeeeally like him? Or do you just like the idea of his asking you out? If you enjoy his company and can handle his casual attitude, OK, I guess. But since you took the time to write, it sounds like this on-again/off-again romance is not totally OK with you, and that's understandable! After all, why should he make all the decisions? Remember that most first loves don't last forever and that it's better to be alone (and available to meet new boys) than to be stuck in a relationship that has run its course.

Growing Up
Is Hard to Do

Chapter 5

"It's fun being a kid, but you're
going to enjoy being a teenager, too."

I have to be honest. Growing up can be tricky! While one friend is playing with Barbies, the other may have boys on the brain. While one friend feels anxious about sleepovers, the other may live for slumber parties. Sometimes a girl feels as though she's not ready to turn into a teen. Other times it's her parents who want her to stay ten forever.

Ten. Teen. The letter "e" is the only difference in how these words look. But there's a huge difference in what they mean.

The message of this chapter is one of patience. Friends and family members need to be patient with one another. People change at different rates, and caring relationships *can* survive a few bumpy patches.

So be patient with each other. And be patient with yourself, too.

You are growing, little by little, ready or not.

Do I have to?

Dear Carol,

Sometimes I feel like I want to grow up and be older, but other times I think I really don't. I like being a kid even though I know that I have to be a teen soon. I want to talk to my mom about it, but she'd probably tell everyone. What should I do?

—Torn

Dear Carol,

Two of my friends made fun of me for buying some new Barbie stuff. They said Barbie is for babies, but it wasn't that long ago that they played Barbies with me.

—Mad

Dear Torn,

Feeling confused is totally normal—especially now. It's fun to be a kid, but you're going to enjoy being a teenager, too, and it's not as if teens aren't allowed to do cartwheels or have snowball fights. Some of my favorite grown-ups still have their child-like enthusiasm. Tell your mom you'd like to talk to her about something personal, and that if she can't keep it to herself, you won't confide in her anymore. As far as friends go, bare your heart to your closest ones. You may find they are thinking along the same lines as you are.

Dear Mad,

There's no rule that says you have to put away Barbie or any doll, blanket, or stuffed animal on any particular birthday. If your friends want to apply nail polish or practice piano instead, fine. You can do that, too. But if they tease you for playing with Barbies, cut them off with confidence. Say, "I still like Barbie," and try not to sound defensive. Act like it's no big deal and, chances are, they'll admire your honesty—and leave you alone.

Is this weird?

Dear Carol,

I'm eleven and I have an imaginary friend. Well, more like an imaginary boyfriend. I know that I'm way too old for this. I've wondered if I have this imaginary boyfriend because I don't get any attention from the boys at school. Or maybe I'm just nuts? As for my imaginary Romeo, I've tried to get rid of him, but when I do, I feel lonely. If my friends knew, they'd laugh so hard.

—Mr. Invisible's Girl

Dear Mr. Invisible's Girl,

You're not nuts. Lots of people have fantasies and ideas about the perfect friend or boyfriend. It doesn't mean that you're kooky. But if you ever find yourself buying two packs of gum—one for you, and one for Romeo—

then I might worry! Sounds like you're well aware that your guy is imaginary—which is a good thing. If this is distracting or tripping you up, confide in an adult you trust rather than a friend. You're right—your friends might not totally understand. Meanwhile, be a little friendlier with real guys, and you *just* might find that Mr. Invisible just kind of fades away.

Dear Carol,

Some of my friends are going to sleepaway camp, but I get really homesick. I try not to think of my parents, but it doesn't help. I can't even stay at my grandmother's without calling home.

—Weirdly Homesick

Dear Homesick,

First off, you're not weird. You're normal, and there's nothing like snuggling in your own bed. Lots of girls get homesick, and not everyone is ready for sleepaway camp. Nevertheless, push yourself to be more independent, because sleepovers are really fun. Next time you go to your grandmother's, pack your teddy and pillow—and try to wait until morning to call home. (Hearing your parents' voices can make girls feel worse, not better.) Maybe your parents can offer a little sleepover-survival reward, like lip gloss or cool stationery. Or maybe they can write you a little note to take with you and you can bring a photo from home. Many girls share your anxieties, but work toward feeling more independent so that you can enjoy your parents at your home and enjoy your friends at their homes.

Dear Carol,

I sleep with a stuffed animal. How can I break apart from my comfort-giver?

—Age Twelve

Dear Age Twelve,

Why should you? You're not the only twelve-year-old who cuddles up with a stuffed animal. Sleeping with an animal for comfort is not like sucking your thumb in public or dragging a blankie around. Give yourself a break! Soon enough, you'll change your ways without even trying. If you still want to break the habit, put your animal on a shelf or at the end of your bed, instead of right next to you. Grab a pillow if you need something to hold. But don't rush yourself—really.

Dear Carol,
My mom calls me nicknames too embarrassing to repeat. I tell her to stop, but she laughs and says, "I can't stop—you're my baby." I've tried not responding to her when she calls me by these "pet names," but it doesn't work.

—Nicknamed

Dear Nicknamed,
Lots of kids are called Lambkins or Sweetie Pie when no one is listening. But if Mom calls you Baby Face or GooGoo Girl in public, that's a bit much. You've already asked her to give it a rest, but try again. Shouting, "Maaahhhaaam, cut it out!" is not ideal. Write her a note: "Dear Mom, I love you, and there is something I want to tell you that is important to me. When you call me X or Y, it embarrasses me a lot and sounds childish, and I want you to see that I'm growing up. Could you please call me Z in public? I like my name! Thanks!"

Dear Carol,
I am twelve (almost thirteen), and I have a big, embarrassing problem. I don't sleep in my bed! My parents are divorced, so I sleep with my mom. At my dad's, I usually cry myself to sleep. I've tried to sleep in my bed millions of times, but I just can't. I get so scared, but I don't even know what I'm scared of. My mom says she wants to take me to see a therapist, but I don't think I need to.

—Scared and Hopeless

Dear Scared,
Although you think you don't need it, a good therapist can help you with this problem. Since your mom wants to take you, why not go? The therapist will help you figure out why you're afraid to separate from your mother at night. You'll move toward understanding that, although your parents left each other, you are not being left alone. Because you are capable of getting to sleep at your dad's (even though it's painful), you already know you can sleep without your mom nearby. Keep thinking about how good it will feel when you are comfortably independent— and how much fun it will be to join friends for sleepovers or slumber parties! Many people have fears, and many conquer them. You can, too.

Dear Carol,

I have a really embarrassing secret. I'm not a geek and I'm not best friends with my parents or anything—but almost every night, my dad reads me to sleep. Like fairy tales and picture books! Am I really weird, immature, or just attached to my inner child?

—Twelve Going on Two

Dear Twelve,
Chill! It's great that your dad reads to you almost every night. Who says parents have to stop reading aloud just because kids can read on their own? You're not weird or immature, and there's nothing wrong with your father-daughter ritual.

Why can't we all grow up at the same time?

Dear Carol,

I just got my ears pierced, but my friend can't get her ears pierced until she's thirteen. We're ten. Every time I mention my ears or earrings, she gets this sad look on her face. I don't know if I should act like it's no big deal, or if I should talk about it with her a lot, as if her ears were pierced, too. I really don't want to hurt her. Please help!

—Sad-eared

Dear Sad-eared,
You are a sensitive friend, so how about being honest? Instead of acting like it's no big deal or acting like her ears are also pierced, just say what you are both thinking: You wish she could have gotten her ears pierced, too. Before long, she will. In the meantime, even though you're really excited, don't talk too much about ears or earrings, but don't feel guilty if the subject comes up.
P. S. I never got my ears pierced—I wear clip earrings and that's fine, too.

Dear Carol,

My best friend and I used to have so much fun together. We played outside, made up stories, acted them out, etc. Last summer, she went to camp and made friends with some girls who go to our school. They totally changed her. Now she wears trendy skirts, tights and sweaters, and wants to read fashion magazines instead of doing the stuff we used to do. Our moms are friends, so they want us to stay friends. She's still really nice, but it's like being with a different person. I've tried talking to her, but she just smiles and says I'm still her friend.

—Where Did She Go?

Dear Where?,

It's hard when friends grow in different directions or at different rates. I'm glad this girl is still nice and friendly toward you (as opposed to being distant and snobby), but I'm sorry you two are out of sync. Give her some space to be her new self, but still hang out occasionally. In the meantime, look around to see if an acquaintance could become a closer friend. Someone on your bus? The new girl at school? While casting around for new buds, don't give up on your original BFF. Who knows? In a few years, the two of you may be going off to camp *together*—or even double-dating!

Dear Carol,

My BFF is starting to like boys. She's always fixing her hair, while the rest of us don't care if our hair looks like it's been in a twister. When she comes over, all she talks about is boys. She's starting to push us away. If I had my way, I would ship boys off to Planet X! I have known her for six years, so I don't really want to dump her.

—Cupid Is Stupid

Dear Cupid Is Stupid,
Then *don't* dump her. Your long-term friendship doesn't have to screech to a halt just because you're going through different phases or have different interests. Boy-crazy girls can be best friends with book-crazy girls or horse-crazy girls or artistic girls or athletic girls. Don't criticize your friend, but next time she goes on and on about the hottie in homeroom, say, "I know you like him, but let's talk about something else for a change." And have a few conversation topics ready—a change in a teacher, a new movie, your guinea pig's babies—you could talk about anything!

Talking it out

Dear Carol,

I'm having trouble. My sister moved to college, and I have no one to talk to about this stage of my life. I don't talk to my mom about it because I am sort of embarrassed.

—Embarrassed

Dear Embarrassed,

There's no need to be embarrassed about growing up. Your body is changing, and that's normal, natural, and healthy. But it is new to you, and therefore it may feel strange and even awkward. Many of your friends are developing now, and they probably feel just as funny and shy about it. Can you confide in them? Or in a school nurse? Or your aunt or grown-up cousin? Can you call your sister at college? And don't give up on your mother. Just say, "Mom, I feel embarrassed about this, but I want to ask you about puberty." There is lots of information in books, magazines, and online, too.

Dear Carol,

My parents can't accept that I've grown up. I like music, MTV, the Internet, boys.... My dad thinks he's "lost" me, but I've just gained other interests, which my parents call "obsessions." How can I get them to accept me?

—Grown Up

Dear Grown Up,

You're not the first girl with new interests and fretting parents. But you *can* stay close to your folks. Talk to them about the novel you're reading in English class, ask about their work, or discuss upcoming family plans. In other words, find common neutral ground instead of expecting to see eye to eye with them about MTV. Your dad is upset because he loves you, and it's hard for parents to watch their children turn into young adults. Reassure him by saying, "Dad, I'm growing up, but I'll always be your daughter. Want to go for a walk or to a movie?" It's natural that you're separating a little, but keep your relationship with your parents healthy by making a point of spending time with them.

Dear Carol,

My parents invade my privacy. They enter my room without asking, they listen in when I'm on the phone, they open my mail, and I bet they check my e-mail, too. It's not fair because I'm a good kid so they shouldn't worry so much.

—Invaded

Dear Invaded,

Time to talk with them. They may *think* they're being responsible parents, but you can tell them that they're taking it too far. Don't scream, "Leave me alone!" Just remind them that they have raised you well and that you're not hiding anything so it hurts when they act like they don't trust you. Be more open with them so they won't get so curious or suspicious. Instead of saying, "I'll be back at six," say, "I'm going to Amanda's to do our art project and I'll be back at six." When a friend comes over, instead of racing to your room and slamming the door, say a quick, "Hi" to your parents. And no double standards! No walking into *their* room without knocking, or reading *their* letters without asking.

P. S. If it's any consolation, a lot of girls have your very same complaint.

Dear Carol,

For my eleventh birthday, I want to have a boy-girl party, but I'm afraid to ask my mom. What should I do?

—Birthday Girl

Dear Birthday Girl,

If you don't ask your mom, you definitely *won't* be having a boy-girl party. So you might as well ask. She probably doesn't want you to invite the whole grade over, so think through your guest list before running it by her. If she freaks, drop the idea, until next year—and don't complain unduly. Girls-only parties are fun, too—and less jittery.

Dear Carol,
I'm eleven, and my mother says I am way too young to date. It's not like I even know any boys, but still, my mother and I always argue about it.

—Wants to Date

Dear Wants to Date,
Save your arguing for later. At eleven (and even twelve, thirteen, and fourteen), very few girls date. When you're older and someone you like asks you out, ask for the go-ahead. Meanwhile, don't spend today fighting about tomorrow.

Dear Carol,
There is a nasty rumor going around about me that isn't true.

—Nasty Rumor

Dear N.R.,
I'm sorry about that rumor, but I bet it will fade as fast as it came—especially since it's not true. Serious people don't take rumors seriously. If you can't just ignore it, talk to your friends about helping defend your reputation, though this sometimes keeps everyone talking longer. Consider these words of Oscar Wilde (1854-1900), *"The only thing worse than getting talked about is not getting talked about."* For now, hold your head high and try to be visible in a positive new way—on stage or in class or on the field. Talk to your parents or older siblings about this, too. They can help reassure you that friends know you by your actions, not by what may have been said about you.

Family Matters

Chapter 6

"You're growing and changing,
and that can mean separating
a bit from your parents."

No wonder world peace seems like an impossible goal. Even harmony on the homefront is pretty hard to pull off.

This chapter is about making the best of your nest.

Some girls get along really well with their parents. But many don't. And sometimes it's the parents who don't get along with each other.

Do you have siblings? Do you fight with them? Wouldn't it be better for everyone if you could stop the fighting—or at least lower the volume on it?

Read on to see how other girls have dealt with family members who ignore them, invade their privacy, battle with them, or battle with each other. There are ways to make your family more peaceful and more fun.

Good luck!

Hey, remember me? Staying tight with sibs

Dear Carol,

My sister is seventeen and she's always on the phone, in the shower, or out with her new boyfriend. I'm tired of it, and sometimes I get angry because she used to like being with me.

—Sad Sis

Dear Sis,

Tell your sister you miss her. Make popcorn and knock on her door to confide in her, or ask her advice about a friend. Leave a note under her pillow saying, "Let's go for a walk this weekend." Or draw a picture of the two of you and slip it under her door. If you gently remind her that you're still around, she may be happy to include you again—at least once in a while. Even if she *is* busier than ever, I bet she still likes being with you.

Dear Carol,

My brother is seven years older, and he doesn't know I exist. I don't expect us to be best friends, but I want him to see I'm not just a little kid.

—Nine

Dear Nine,

Talk to your brother. If you have a problem you'd like help with, ask for his opinion. He may be flattered, and it will help him see you are growing up. Suggest that you walk the dog or play a computer game together. As you get older, the age gap will seem smaller and smaller.

Dear Carol,

My little sister won't stop barging into my room, listening in on my phone conversations, or just being mean. I've tried all sorts of things, but she won't stop. What should I do?
—Little Sister Problems

Dear Little Sister Problems,

Hang in there! Here's what I want to know: Is your sister being bratty because she's mean or because she likes (even idolizes) you and is desperate for your attention? Instead of yelling at her for invading your privacy, try a new approach. Play a board game together, bake brownies, or ask her about her friends. Then when you need time by yourself, tell her—without sounding harsh—that you need time for yourself, but you'll play with her again another time. Worth a try!

Dear Carol,

My older brother is going away all summer, and I'm going to miss him tons!
—Separated in Summer

Dear Separated,

He'll be back! You can stay tight with your brother by writing, calling, or e-mailing. Go wild and send him a care package—a batch of extra gooey brownies with chocolate chips (his weakness), the latest book by his favorite author, a mini photo album, a CD, or a T-shirt. Can you visit him one weekend? The two of you could have a blast!

Privacy problems

Dear Carol,

I have a little sister and I never get any privacy. She drives me nuts!

—Never Alone

Dear Never,

Siblings come in handy during a crisis or when you want company at odd hours. But they *can* be a nuisance when they don't get that you need some solo time. When your sister bugs you, do you scream, "Get out of my face, you little dork," as you slam the door? Or do you watch her set up Candyland while silently screaming your head off? It's time to speak up directly but politely. Say, "I'll play one quick game, but then I need to be alone to read." If the two of you share a room, ask your mom or dad about letting you have a corner of the basement or attic to escape to every once in a while. Perhaps you can find a place in your backyard where you can be alone—a hammock or treehouse. Your little sister looks up to you and likes to be with you, and that's nice. But you *are* entitled to some time alone.

Dear Carol,

My sister and I share a room. It's never been a problem until recently. Lately we always get on each other's nerves. I sleep on the top bunk and, if I even so much as sit on her bed, she gets mad at me. And she's always borrowing my headbands and using my Discman. My parents say I shouldn't hope we'll move because we won't.

—Unhappy Roommate

Dear Unhappy Roommate,

Sisters are forever, so you might as well think of ways to improve things. Can you set a few rules to make getting along easier? No borrowing without asking is a good place to start. Can you get a comfortable chair so you won't need to sit on her bed? Maybe label some shelves and drawers for her stuff, others for yours? Sharing a room isn't easy. But since you'll *both* be happier if you argue less, it's worth talking about what works and what doesn't. Come up with ideas of your own, then ask your parents for suggestions and support.

Can I make her/him disappear?

Dear Carol,

I wish my little sister would go away. When I tell her that, she does this fake cry and tells on me. Then I tell her to shut up, and she screams. How will I ever learn to deal with her?

—Devil Sister

Dear Sister,

At least you recognize that something has to change. Here's my wild and crazy idea: Imagine for thirty seconds that your little sister is a friend's little sister. She might not seem soooooo bad, right? You might even say, "I like the way you play piano," or, "Cute barrettes," or, "What's your new doll's name?"

Now try it. Shock your sister with a compliment. Challenge her to a board game. Play a duet on the piano. Or, just be silent instead of mean-mouthed. You'll always have quarrels, but you are old enough to quit lashing out at her.

Dear Carol,

My new baby sister is a pain. She gets all the attention. My mom always plays with her, and I feel left out. My dad is always out of town, so there's no one to talk to.

—Left Out

Dear Left Out,

Babies need lots of attention since they can't eat, drink, or take care of going to the bathroom on their own. Even though you're grown up, you deserve and need attention, too. What to do? Tell your mom you love her and wish you could spend some time alone with her. It would be ideal if your mom could get a sitter to watch the baby while you two get ice cream or catch a movie. But if finding child care is impossible, you and your mom can still make dinner together while the baby naps. Or go for a walk and take turns pushing the stroller. Someday you and your little sister will be buddies, but for now, let your busy mom (and dad when he's around) know you miss them. It's also easier if you make more plans with your friends.

Dear Carol,

My mother thinks I'm a built-in baby-sitter for my baby brother. I'm not! He's a toddler and he's cute and all, but why should I invite him to hang with my friends?

—Baby Brother Blue

Dear Blue,

Tell your mother how you feel. Tell her you love your bro and you're willing to baby-sit sometimes, but that you and your friends can't play or talk when he's tagging along. Say that before or after you spend an afternoon with friends, you'll spend half an hour playing or reading to your brother, but that you really need some time on your own. If you tell this to your mom calmly—without huffing or sighing—she might see things your way. Remember, too, that before you know it, he'll have friends of his own, and your playing with him now is building a sibling bond you both will enjoy for years.

Hello?! Getting your parents to pay attention to you

Dear Carol,

Everything revolves around my sister's schedule. Between her horseback riding lessons, tennis practice, drum lessons, and track practices, I can only do flute class. I want to play a sport, but my mom doesn't have time. How can I tell my mom it doesn't seem fair?

—Tired of Being a Couch Potato

Dear Tired,

Fair? Sorry, but family life is *not* always fair. Some sibs get extra attention because of actvities, illness, or something temporary like applying to college. Nevertheless, you *are* entitled to talk to your mom. Try, "Mom, I'd like to take up a sport." Tell her you know her schedule is complicated but that you love the confidence sports can offer. (How could she resist?) Also, look into carpooling with others to get to and from practice.

Dear Carol,

I feel like my brother Justin gets more attention than I do. My parents hardly notice I'm around.

—Ignored

Dear Ignored,
Most parents mean well but are often so overwhelmed with adult responsibilities that they aren't always in tune with what their kids are feeling. What to do? First, what *not* to do—don't start doing things you know your parents disapprove of just to get noticed. You want attention, but not negative attention. A good way to get parents to deal with you is to deal with them. Start conversations. Ask a question that shows you want to talk, like, "How was work today?"—anything just to get the ball rolling. Or just be direct. Instead of feeling hurt that they didn't ask about your art project, announce, "I want to show you my artwork. The teacher liked it." Finally, why not tell them straight out what you're feeling? If you say, "You love Justin more!" they'll say, "Nonsense!" But if you say, "I feel as though you spend more time with Justin than me," they'll most likely listen—and try to change their ways.

Dear Carol,

My dad is almost always on the computer. When he is off, he spends time with my brothers. What am I going to do? I feel empty.

—Needs Love

Dear N.L.,
Tell your dad you miss him and want to spend time with him. Be specific and say you would love to play cards, go bicycling, see a movie, or whatever he might like. Set up a date—whether it's tonight after dinner, or Saturday morning. Keep pressing your dad without whining, and see if you can make a weekly date of it. Maybe every Sunday, you two could make pancakes together or go bowling. A few dads are hopeless, but you'd be doing yours a big favor if you could get him to look *away* from his computer screen—and *at* his growing daughter. One more idea: You could send him a sweet e-mail saying that you miss him and want to hang out with him!

Dear Carol,

My dad doesn't care about the things my brother and I do, or our awards. How do I get him to appreciate our success more?

—Father Troubles

Dear Father Troubles,

I'm sorry your dad doesn't show pride in you and your brother. Maybe the two of you could write a letter to your dad explaining how hard you work to get awards and that you would feel really good if you knew he were proud. Tell him you have a meet/performance/recital and that it would mean a lot to you if he were to attend. If your dad stays blind to your accomplishments, it will hurt. But you're not alone. Lots of kids have inattentive fathers—which is a shame for the kids *and* dads. Some kids look to godparents and other relatives for extra affection. Have you told your grandparents about your achievements? They might want to hear every detail. A teacher, coach, uncle, or close friend could also provide pats on the back and help you stay motivated. Here's hoping you and your brother get the encouragement and congratulations you deserve. But it's important that you continue to achieve for the sense of accomplishment it brings to you—not anyone else. Keep boosting up each other, too.

Dear Carol,

Lately, my mom always seems so busy and preoccupied. This might sound dorky, but I miss when she used to hang out with me. Should I tell her how I feel?

—Missing Mom

Dear M.M.,

Why not? But instead of complaining that she's never around, see if you can find moments when she might welcome a little company. For instance, if she's racing to a meeting or talking on the phone, don't suddenly tell her about your grade in History and expect her full attention. But if she's unloading the dishwasher or folding laundry or driving you home, she'd probably love to hear what's going on. Even if your mom is not asking about your life, go ahead and volunteer information about what you are up to. Finding the right time and right tone makes a difference. And don't forget to ask about what's on her mind, too.

They just don't understand!

Dear Carol,

I go to a new school, and there's one girl I love and one girl I hate. Problem is, my parents like the parents of the girl I hate. They want me to invite both girls to do something with us next weekend. I don't want to!

—Love-hate

Dear Love-hate,

Try not to hate the one classmate or anyone else for that matter. This doesn't mean you have to like everyone, but it's so much easier to just not deal with people you're not especially fond of. Be civil or simply avoid her, because hating her wastes a lot of time and energy. Tell your parents it's great they like her family so much, but that you have given it a shot and the two of you are like oil and water. You're old enough to choose your own friends. Help your parents respect your decision by being clear and calm about your feelings. Stomping your feet and exclaiming, "I hate her!" won't help your cause. Likely, there's some sticky parental social stuff going on, and your parents might be put in a bind if you refuse to befriend this girl. Assure them that you won't be mean to her or anything, you just don't want to be friends. Then suggest a compromise for the weekend. Can your parents see her parents without the kids tagging along? Hopefully, if you don't use words like *Hate,* or *Forget it,* or *No way!,* your folks just may listen.

Dear Carol,

I made a new friend who is also my locker partner. We see movies, have sleepovers, and do other stuff together. The problem is that my whole family dislikes her a lot. I can see why, because when I'm around her, I act bad and different, and sometimes I don't listen to my parents.

—True Friends?

Dear True,

Why do you act differently when she's around? Wouldn't she like you for your real self? If she's getting you to misbehave, no wonder your family worries about her influence on you. If you want to remain true friends with this girl, you must first be true to yourself and not make changes just because of her. Otherwise, you can see why your parents may not want to welcome her into your home—and then you and she will both lose out.

Dear Carol,

My parents don't seem to believe me anymore. I tell them my little sister throws stuff and my little brother cheats at games. They give me "the look" as if I'm lying. How can I prove that I don't tell lies?

—Fed Up

Dear Fed Up,

Do your parents *really* think you're lying? Ask them what they mean when they give you "the look." They might just wish you, your brother, and your sister would work out arguments on your own. Call a truce with your sister, and tell your brother you won't play if he is going to cheat.

Dear Carol,

I want to try kickboxing, judo, or fencing, but my mom thinks they are horrid sports that promote violence. I think they would be fun. What can I do?

—Karate Kid

Dear Karate Kid,

Point out to your mother that these sports can teach you discipline, strengthening techniques, and confidence to defend yourself if necessary. Make sure she knows you're not planning on a career as a fencer but that you'd just like to try the sport—like you would for any other after-school activity. And rather than expecting your mom to do the footwork for something that doesn't appeal to her, find out for yourself where and when the classes meet. Finally, if you have a friend who also wants to take these sports, talk to her (and your mom) about signing up and carpooling together. If you act mature and respectful, your mom may come around.

Dear Carol,

All my parents care about are grades. Last report card, I got a C in math. I thought they were going to kill me! Whenever I try to talk to them about how I feel, they yell at me. My mom is not as bad as my dad. I know they care about my education, but they hurt my feelings.

—Sick of It

Dear Sick of It,

If you want to tell your parents how you feel but can't do it in person, write them a note. Did you get a good grade they forgot to praise? Say so. Tell them you'd like to hear when they're proud of you, not just when they're disappointed. But remember that they care about your education because they care about you and your future. Might it help if you get a math tutor? Maybe a high school student can bring you up to speed without charging too much. Your math teacher can probably recommend someone. It's hard to excel in school when you feel pressure on all sides. But psych yourself up now for a change in strategy. Plan to move up to the front row, keep an organized assignment pad, find a quiet place to work, do your best, and your grades will go up, guaranteed. Not only will your parents be pleased, but you'll feel good about it, too.

Battles with parents

Dear Carol,

My mom and I don't get along. She always screams at me, so I yell back because it's the only thing that comes to mind at the time. I know it's not right, but I have no other defense. My friend says I'm not very pleasant to her. Can you give me some advice? I'd really like to get along.

—Yelling

Dear Yelling,

Sounds like you and she are locked in a pattern. Kudos to you for asking how to break it—that's a big step in the right direction. To improve matters, tell your mom (in person or in a note) that you want to get along better. Or simply be nicer to her, which should help her be nicer to you. Compliment her cooking or her funky new earrings. Thank her for buying microwave popcorn. Ask about her day, and tell her about yours. Finally, if you know what sets her off (loud music, talking back, snacking before dinner), don't push those buttons—you'll be doing yourself a favor, honest! Could be she is unhappy about something that has nothing to do with you, but I'm sure she, like you, would love your relationship to be better. Make that your common goal.

Dear Carol,

My mom and I fight all the time. It's about something different every day. The other day, she was mad at me for not wearing a certain pair of pants. She has no idea how hard it is being a tween. I hate when we fight, but I can't stand her sometimes.
—Troubled Tween

Dear Carol,

I'm mean to my mom a lot. I don't try to be. The words just come out. My parents have been divorced since I was two, so I'm used to being how I am. I'm twelve now. Do you think the divorce triggered it?
—Mean (but Not Trying to Be)

Dear T.T.,
Being a tween is fun—and hard. Just as being a mom is fun—and hard. I'm sure she hates the fights, too. You could say, "Mom, I'll wear those pants this weekend, but let's not fight over it now, OK?" Need more ideas?
1. Avoid starting sentences with, "Everyone else..." because that pushes parents' buttons.
2. Agree sometimes, and say, "That's true," or, "Good idea," or, "I see what you mean."
3. Give occasional compliments—even saying, "You look nice," or, "The pasta is good," can lift her mood.
4. Be as grown up as you can. When you act like a grown-up, your mom is more likely to treat you the way you want to be treated.
5. Don't try to have the last word. It's not easy to change patterns, but it *is* possible.

Dear Mean (but Not Trying to Be),
Since your parents divorced ten years ago, I doubt the breakup is the sole reason for your harsh words. You're growing and changing, and that can mean separating a bit from your mom. But, as you realize, that doesn't justify rudeness. Plus, whenever you're mean, others (even moms) tend to act mean in return. So make an effort to be nicer—not candy cane sweet, but at least polite. If you slip up, quickly offer an apology, in person or in writing. If you feel like giving your mom a compliment, don't hold back. Kind words can go a long, long way.

My family is different

Dear Carol,

I have a brother who is a slow learner. He has great friends but, when we're out, people make fun of him. Whenever he hears names being yelled at him, he is deeply hurt. What should I do?

—Distressed

Dear Distressed,

You are a wonderful sister and good person. Next time people are mean, say to your brother, "What fools! Don't pay attention to them," or, "They don't know that you're worth a hundred of them." The support and love of a sister can outweigh the criticism and jibes of strangers. And I bet you have already educated more people than you realize.

Dear Carol,

I live in a home where we do foster care. I used to get along fine with the kids we took in, but now I can't. Our new foster girl is too hard to deal with. We started off on the wrong foot, and now she has a lot of attitude and is rude and mean. She also calls my mom "Mom." Whenever she makes me upset, I go to my room, turn off all the lights, turn my radio up really loud, and go into my closet to cry. I try to talk to my mom, but she doesn't understand and doesn't always let me tell my side of the story.

—Alone

Dear Alone,

You come from a caring family. Of course it's hard for you to share your mom, especially when you're at an age when you may need to talk to her more. Why not show your mom this letter? You can confess that you wrote it, or say that you sometimes feel this way. Some reassuring one-on-one time can make a real difference. You deserve it, so ask for it. I hope you can also try to befriend the troubled girl. Can you talk to your school counselor about your very understandable feelings?

Dear Carol,

I'm ten and I was adopted. My science teacher keeps talking about heritage and family trees, and when she does, it makes me feel alone.
—Different

Dear Different,

These days, how can you describe a typical family? I'm certain a lot of your classmates have nontraditional families, and I'm sorry your teacher is not more sensitive. Enlighten her after class by politely saying that since you were adopted, some of her statements about families make you feel like an outsider. Tell her you'd love for her to explore all different types of families in class. By the way, I hope you feel at home in your family, and that you're totally comfortable talking to your adoptive parents about your feelings, which are perfectly natural.

Dear Carol,

I'm afraid my mom might be gay. Ever since my parents got divorced, my brother has suspected it. Now I do, too. I can't talk to her about it. She avoids embarrassing talks.
—Scared

Dear Scared,

Divorce is hard on everybody, especially at first. After divorce, many women spend more time with their women friends. Why? Because they may feel awkward hanging out with happily married couples. Don't assume your mom is gay just because she goes out with women a lot. If, however, it turns out your mom is gay, please know that this should not change how you and she get along. Other girls and guys have parents who are gay, and what matters isn't really who else your parent loves, but how your parent loves you. I hope you and your mom can talk about all this (embarrassing or not) because it's no fun to be scared.

Surviving divorce

Dear Carol,

My parents are divorced, and I live with my dad. My aunt constantly says, "Your mom is a BAD mother." It's not true. I told my mom, and she said to tell my aunt to be quiet, but I'm afraid my aunt will start yelling at me. What should I do?

—Afraid of Aunt

Dear Afraid,
After a divorce, it's best if kids can still love and respect both parents. Your aunt may love you *and* loathe your mom, but it doesn't help you to hear your mom being bad-mouthed. Ask your dad to ask his sister to stop trashing your mother.

Dear Carol,

My dad and my mom just separated, and I think they might divorce. My dad has met someone else. On Saturday, my mom complained he was "on a hot date with his girlfriend." My mom cries and has meltdowns a lot. Sometimes she asks my dad to come home and he doesn't. Other times he acts like he wants to come home and she won't let him. My dad is getting a new apartment and taking some of our furniture. He hasn't said anything to me, but he has said a lot of mean things to my mom. I'm mad at him, but I'm supposed to love him and miss him, too. How can I do both?

—The Girl with Separated Parents

Dear Girl,
It's awful when parents turn on each other, and I really hope things work out. Some parents who separate do get back together, but most do not. You can be mad but also love and miss your dad—though maybe not at the exact same second. Relationships with family members are full of mixed feelings. Lots of kids feel both love and anger toward their parents. While you can't control what your parents do, you *can* keep busy so you won't be in the thick of things at home. And remember that no matter what's going on between your parents, they both love you.

Dear Carol,

When I was three, my parents divorced. Now I'm eleven, and I haven't seen my dad since I was five. I call him, but he rarely talks to me. He is supposed to pick me up every other weekend but never does. Does this mean he doesn't love me?

—Eleven

Dear Eleven,

First off, you are definitely not the only girl in this situation—sad but true. Though your dad's actions are very hurtful, don't ever blame yourself for his indifference. It's probably time you accept that he is never going to win the Father of the Year award. And while your dad surely loves you in his own way, he's obviously not very good at showing it or being there for you. This is his terrible shortcoming. Give yourself a pat on the back for managing without him for half a dozen years. Step away from the pain by accepting that it's unlikely he'll change his ways anytime soon. What adults *are* in your life? I hope your mom is good to you and that you have a relative, grandparent, teacher, or friend who gives back to you when you reach out. It might help to talk to a school counselor, too.

Dear Carol,

My mom hasn't visited me for a year. She lives an hour away, and I'm afraid to call because her new husband might answer. My aunt and grandmother spend time with me. I'm grateful, but it's not the same.

—Momless

Dear Momless,

I'm sorry your mom is not there for you. Can you talk to your aunt or grandmother about her? Say, "I really appreciate all you do for me, but do you know what's going on with my mom?" I encourage you to phone her again. If your stepfather answers, say, "Hi, how are you? May I please speak with my mother?" You're *allowed*! I hope your mom comes around. If not, you need to accept this difficult situation. It's no fun to want more than someone else is willing to give.

Dear Carol,

My parents are divorced, and I live with my dad. I see my mom every other weekend. I'm happy the way I'm living now, but my mom wants me to live at her house. She just finished school and has a job. I told her I don't want to live with her, but she insists. My teacher even said I should live with my mom. I love my mom and like seeing her, but I'm happy where I am now.

—Tug-of-War

Dear Tug,
Laws differ from state to state, but it seems to me that if your dad has custody and you're happy where you are, things are settled. What caused your teacher to get involved? Did your mom influence her? Does she distrust your dad? Ask if you're curious, but the point is this: If you and your dad are content where you are—and are on the right side of the law—you don't have to move.

Parent dating dilemmas

Dear Carol,

My parents have been divorced for a while. My dad is remarried, but my mom is not. Recently, my mom broke up with someone who is really nice. Now I feel sad, and I wish my mom did not break up with him. I wish I were a normal kid. Do you think I can get them back together?

—Sad

Dear Sad,
Probably not. But I think you are as normal a kid as everybody else, and I think your mom, like you, may also be feeling sad—even if she initiated the breakup. Why don't you two make some plans together? You both may be feeling alone, so this could be a period of closeness for you. You can even ask about the breakup. Talking about it may make you both feel better. But after you have your heart-to-heart, tell her you know she'll meet another great person because *she's* a great person. And give her a hug. Moms need hugs and kind words as much as kids do!

Dear Carol,

Lately, I've been feeling left out of my dad's life. Ever since he got a new girlfriend, I feel she and I have to compete for his attention. It's very hard to talk to him because he's not a full-time father.

—Needs Attention, Too

Dear Needs,

Ouch. I get a lot of letters like yours, and it makes me wish I could write to the dads and not just the daughters. Since your father can't read your mind, you'll have to tell him how you feel. Don't say, "You pay more attention to your new girlfriend than to me." Instead try, "Dad, I miss you. I don't see you often enough, so when we do get together it means a lot to me if we can do something, just the two of us. What do you think?" I hope he realizes he's lucky to have a daughter who loves him. If all else fails, leave this book open on his desk with a Post-it that says, "I confess—I sometimes feel this way."

Dear Carol,

Everything in my life seems to go wrong. My parents got divorced and now my mom is always asking me what she should wear on dates. I feel like we switched places. I mean, she's going out and I'm staying in. Shouldn't it be the other way around?

—Staying Home

Dear Staying Home,

There is no law that says you and your mom can't both have a social life! If you wish you were going out on weekends, try making plans with your friends and take the initiative to find out about movies and parties. As for watching your mom prepare for a big night out, it's natural that this stirs up mixed emotions for you. There may always be a tiny part of you that wishes your own parents had stayed happily-ever-after. Do you have a friend, sibling, or counselor to discuss this with? If you want to talk to your mom directly, say, "Mom, I'm happy for you, but I have to admit, it's a little weird for me to see you dating." Clearing the air beats feeling sorry for yourself. And believe me, in a few years, your weekends will be busier, too.

Stepfamilies

Dear Carol,

My mom remarried last year, and we all went on vacation afterward. I saw this sweater I really wanted, and it was on sale. But my mom wouldn't buy it for me. Later, she bought my stepsister a sweater that wasn't on sale. I felt so left out, and I said, "It's not fair. You hardly know her, and you bought her something instead of your own daughter."

—Upset

Dear Upset,

I can see why you're upset. You're adjusting to a lot of changes, and it's not easy to accept a stepdad and stepsister. It's especially tough to watch your mom accept and love them. Yet, it's also understandable that your mom is being generous to her stepdaughter. Your goal right now is to become a combined family—not to go on forever with a "me versus them" attitude. New families don't just fall into place immediately—major changes take a lot of work from everyone. As important as it is for your mom to make your stepfather and stepsister feel involved in your family life, it's not OK for her to ignore your feelings. Say, "Mom, I know how much this family means to you. I'm doing my best to make everything work. But it's hard, and I feel overlooked. I miss you, and I'd like just us to do something fun. Maybe Saturday morning?"

Dear Carol,

My stepmom is pregnant. I don't want her to have a baby. It's going to ruin my life! What can I do?

—Ruined

Dear Ruined,

Since you can't change the situation, try changing your attitude. Yes, the new baby might shake things up a bit. And, yes, you might feel overlooked or jealous at first. Your feelings are very natural, so why not tell your dad or stepmom you're excited about the baby, but nervous, too? Or suggest to your dad, for instance, that on Saturday mornings, you could help take care of the baby, but on Saturday afternoons, you and he could have father-daughter time and go to a movie, out bowling, or to lunch. Remember, that noisy infant will turn into a cute tot and could one day become a sweet sib and then a lifelong friend.

Dear Carol,

My stepsister doesn't like the way I dress. She says, "You can't wear that," or, "You have to change." She thinks she can boss me around just because she is a year older. My stepmother doesn't like my style, either. I know this because sometimes she gives me weird looks.

—Outcast with a Cause

Dear Outcast,

If you feel like wearing something, wear it. Don't do it to please or displease your stepsister or stepmother—or anyone else. What really bugs your stepsister may not be your sense of fashion, but having to share her mom with you. Blended family life can be tricky. Hopefully, you two can find a way to get along. Instead of defending yourself, boost your stepsister up with a compliment. Tell her you like her outfit or that you envy her handwriting. Treat her as a friend (not a rival) and, believe it or not, at some point she will follow suit.

Dear Carol,

Ever since my mom got remarried, she pays all of her attention to my stepdad, and is always mad at my brothers and sisters and me for no reason. Well, we do fight a lot, but still...I'm starting to want to live with my dad.

—Hurt

Dear Hurt,

It must have been hard when your parents first split up, and then hard all over again when your mom remarried and suddenly became devoted to your stepdad. You're in the middle of a difficult time, but things can get easier. First, talk to your mom. Don't yell or accuse. Just tell her you'd really like to spend private time with her. Tell her you understand she and your stepdad need adult time, but ask her to consider how to get your family to feel like a family again. Can you and your stepdad work on having your own relationship? Are there things you like about him? If so, ask him if he wants to do something with you. He'd probably like to get along with his instant kids. Your siblings and you are surely fighting more than normal because of all the tension in the house. But you guys are in this together, so you might as well try to talk out your feelings with one another. As for living with your dad, it may be a possibility or maybe it's not practical. For starters, who has custody? Find out more if you need to. In the meantime, telling your mom that you love and miss her is a good way to start restoring family harmony.

Dear Carol,

My little brother is just three months old. Whenever he starts crying, my dad starts telling my mom what to do—and sometimes even yells at her. She ends up crying, which makes me cry. I usually go in my room when this happens, but sometimes I feel like I just can't take it anymore. What should I do?

—Big Sister Blues

Dear Big Sis:

Babies are adorable, but they're demanding. If you say, "Dad, don't yell at Mom," that probably won't help. But what do you think would happen if you said, "Let's not all get upset just because the baby is upset"? In general, when parents act like children, you can either go into your room or try to help. Why not offer to hold or rock the baby? Or offer sympathy. Ask, "Was I that loud when I was little?" and give your mom a hug.

Dear Carol,

My dad is such a baby. Every time he gets mad, he threatens to leave the house. He also blames me for things I don't do. What should I do?

—My Dad Should Be in Diapers

Dear M.D.S.B.I.D.,

Adults sometimes act childish. I'm sorry your dad's frustration and unhappiness are poisoning your home life. Stay out of his way when he's upset, and try to treat him with respect, whether you think he's earned it or not! If he senses his daughter thinks he's a big baby, he might continue to act like one. His tantrums are *not* your fault. But by acting mature and civil, maybe you can help him do the same. People often do what is expected of them. That's why it's important to try not to lose faith in each other. By the way, sometimes adults, like kids, go through bad times, and then things really do get better again. If possible, talk to your mom or dad about what's going on. Ideally, your whole family should get some counseling.

Dear Carol,

My dad died when I was nine. And now my mom has a boyfriend, but he's a jerk. He only pays attention to me when he needs something done. He's always with my brother, and they leave me out. He blames me for stuff I don't even do. And get this, he got mad at me one time and threw a plate of food at me! I mean, I feel alone all the time. What should I do?
—Mom's Boyfriend Is a Jerk

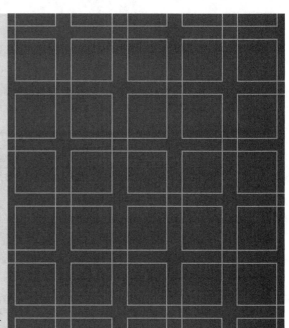

Dear M.B.I.A.J.,

I'm so sorry that your father died. It's hard to bravely carry on after a parent dies—and it can be especially hard when the other parent is dating someone you could do without. Have you told your mom how you feel? Don't tell your mom that her boyfriend is a jerk—but *do* calmly and maturely tell her how you feel. Tell her specific instances of when you've felt ignored or unfairly blamed. Maybe she can talk with her boyfriend. In the meantime, is there any way to improve your relationship with this man? Maybe you can find his good side (it sounds like you've already found his bad side). It may help to pretend that he's a friend's father and treat him as if he were. Be courteous and polite. If he's smart, he'll get the idea and treat you with a little respect—nobody says you two have to be best friends. It might not be easy, but if you compliment him or make him a surprise gift, you might get some of that kindness back. (If not, and he throws another plate of food, talk to your mom and/or to a counselor!) Finally, since you are feeling alone, think about what you can add to your own life. A lot of school sports and extracurricular activities can go a long way in keeping you happily involved elsewhere.

Dear Carol,

My mom may lose her job. If she does, I want to make my own money. I mean, even now, when she has a job, it's hard for her to support our family. I'm only ten. What can I do?

—Worried Daughter

Dear Worried,

Your situation is difficult. Fact is, ten-year-olds can't do much to make money. Later you can walk dogs, baby-sit, flip burgers. For now though, be helpful at home and tell your mom you appreciate how hard she works for you. Emotional support from a daughter is worth gold. And keep your eye on your future. With your practical and mature attitude, your career options will be bright. If your mom does end up out of work, you may want to speak to a relative, teacher, or trusted adult friend about what to do. I hope things work out for you.

Dear Carol,

I'm worried about my parents' jobs. My friend's mom was "let go" and, even though the economy is supposed to be getting better, I'm still worried. I think my dad is worried, too.

—Worried

Dear Worried,

Rather than worrying alone, talk to your dad so he can either calm your fears or let you know exactly what's going on. Even when a parent loses a job, things can work out for the better in the long run. Some people who lose their jobs eventually find work they like even more. And some enjoy spending time between jobs doing family things. If you've noticed your parents talking about money issues more than usual, be sensitive and don't beg for a new computer or rattle on about wanting to go to sleepover camp next summer.

Dear Carol,

My mom smokes and I know how bad it is for her, so I wish she would stop. I've tried talking to her, but she says that it's not my concern. It *is* though. Not only does it hurt her, but if I wanted to breathe in smoke all day, I would be a chimney sweep.

—Up in Smoke

Dear Up in Smoke,
It's hard to break a habit—and even harder to break someone *else's* habit. Tell your mom you want her to stay healthy and hope she can quit, or at least smoke less. Say that if she *must* smoke, would she mind going outside or sticking to just one room? Say please. Be encouraging. Hug, don't nag. And consider telling her that for every day she doesn't smoke, you'll write her a poem, make her a bracelet, help with a chore, give her a gold star, or something else.
P. S. Although your intentions are honorable, results are not guaranteed.

Dear Carol,

Last year at Christmas, my father's dad died. My dad cried in front of all our relatives. He was really upset. I think he still hasn't finished dealing with it. This year we are spending Christmas with my dad's mom, and I think it might be sad.

—Help!

Dear Help!
I doubt Christmas will be sad, but it may be poignant and bittersweet. Don't be afraid to share a memory or say, "I miss Grandpa, too." If your father cries, it's because it takes a long time to feel better after you lose someone. In many ways, you're lucky to have a father who is able to express his love and sorrow. If your memories of your grandfather are happy, say this to your dad. It may be a real comfort to him.

Dear Carol,

I think my mother is depressed but I don't think it's too serious. She talks less than she used to at home, but when we go out, she's as talkative as she always was. Is she going through a mid-life crisis? How can I confront her about this?

—Worried

Dear Worried,

It's thoughtful of you to be aware of your mom's feelings. Instead of "confronting" her, try to be extra talkative and helpful right now. Join her when she's stirring soup, deal out a game of cards, and offer up stories about friends or teachers. If you like, ask if something is bothering her. It's also okay to be yourself—you don't have to be a model child 24/7. But I'm sure she'd appreciate your extra love and support while something else (work? relationships?) is bringing her down.

Dear Carol,

I miss my grandmother (my mother's mother). We got along really well. She died a year ago. Shouldn't I be over her by now?

—Missing

Dear Missing,

When someone you love dies, you never 100 percent get over that person. You accept the death, but you don't forget the love you had. I'm sure your grandmother cherished the relationship she had with you. And I'm sorry that relationship didn't last longer. But the memories you have are safe within you, and you can think about your grandmother whenever you want. At first, revisiting memories is painful, but as time passes, you'll be able to recall the past with smiles instead of wistfulness. Talk to your mom about your grandmother. She may welcome the opportunity to talk about her mom and to share memories with you. And she probably finds comfort in knowing that your grandmother lives on in you.

Who Is Dear Carol?

Dear Carol,

It seems like you always know the right thing to say. How'd you get to be such an expert on all this girl stuff? And another thing, who are you?

—Give Me the Scoop

Dear Scoop,

Good questions! I *hope* I always know the right thing to say. I love giving girls advice and I'm proud that I've been the *Girls' Life* guru ever since its first issue back in 1994.

How do I know what to say? First of all, I remember being a girl and a teen. I kept a dozen diaries of my own roller-coaster adolescence, and at Yale, I studied psychology, sociology, and literature. I worked hard at figuring out what makes healthy, happy relationships—and what doesn't. At nineteen, I began writing for *Seventeen* magazine, and in my twenties, I wrote my first book, *Girltalk: All the Stuff Your Sister Never Told You* (HarperCollins 1985, revised '92, '97).

Once *Girltalk* was published, I started getting tons of mail. Friendship meltdowns, teacher troubles, sibling spats, crush craziness, body questions—I've heard it all. *Girltalk* is now in print in many languages, and I've written other advice books including *Private and Personal*, *For Girls Only*, and *For Teens Only*. I've also talked about girls on the *Today Show*, *48 Hours*, *The View*, *Oprah*, and *Montel Williams*. Each year, I visit schools and get to know as many girls as I can. I like making up stories, too. My novels are *The Diary of Melanie Martin* (set in Italy), *Melanie Martin Goes Dutch* (set in Holland), and she's on the move again in *With Love From Spain, Melanie Martin*.

Am I a know-it-all? No way! I get stumped. Who doesn't? But when I don't know the answer, I consult experts and do research until I come up with whatever info I need to help a girl—or, better yet, lots of girls.

What else? Well, I live in New York City with my husband, our daughters Emme and Elizabeth, and our little rabbit, Honey Bunny. Want to learn more (or see some family photos)? Visit www.carolweston.com.

Catch You Later

Thank you for reading this book! I hope you enjoyed the letters from girls and the answers from Carol, and I hope they gave you some insights, ideas, and encouragement.

The growing up years in your life can have bad days, but admit it, deep down, it's pretty great to be your age, isn't it? You're not worried about wrinkles or car payments or health insurance, and you almost *always* get to have lunch with friends. Okay, so maybe the cafeteria serves nothing but fish sticks and clumpy pasta, but *still*, you can place your tray right next to a best friend's—or possibly even a crush's!

I leave you with two quotes to think about. Eleanor Roosevelt (1884–1962) said, *"No one can make you feel inferior without your consent"* which means, roughly: Don't let the goons get you down. And Maya Angelou (1928–)said, *"Life loves to be taken by the lapel and told, 'I'm with you kid. Let's go!'"* which translates into: Figure out where you're headed, and take off in that direction!

Here's hoping you get where you're going. Enjoy these years and make the most of them. Oh, and be yourself, too. After all, if *you* won't be you, who will?

XOXO,

Karen Bokram
Editor-in-Chief, *GL Magazine*